T0087247

RUDIMENTAL ETUDES AND WARM-UPS
Covering all 40 Rudiments

Written by
Kit Chatham, Steve Murphy, & Joe Testa

Dedicated with much love to
Sandy Feldstein
(1940 – 2007)

Special Thanks to: Rob Grad, Scotty Bahler, Troy Wollwage, John Wittmann, Prudence Elliott, Aaron Felske, Jim Petercsak, Rob Shanahan, and SmartMusic

Cover Artwork: Rob Grad - IdeasInc.biz
Book Design and Engraving: Kit Chatham

TABLE OF CONTENTS:

INTERMEDIATE

RUDIMENTAL ETUDES

[PREFACE]

Sandy Feldstein helped to mentor and cultivate the careers of so many in the music industry. His positive influence reached hundreds of people throughout his life; but, for the select few within his inner circle, he had a very profound and intimate impact. I thank God everyday for the blessing to have been able to learn from, interact with, and love him as teacher, friend, and musical father figure.

Similar to many percussion educational works, it is through him that the **Principal Percussion Series** was born. Originally a project he and I were to work on together, his untimely passing left it my hands to finish. Knowing the scope of the project, I brought in two of my friends whom I felt are not only fine musicians, but well-respected educators in their own fields: Kit Chatham and Steve Murphy. With Kit and Steve's help, I believe we accomplished the original directive as outlined by SmartMusic, all the while keeping a bit of Sandy's essence through each page.

Rudimental Etudes and Warm-ups is just what the title implies. There are three books – each dedicated to a different difficulty level: Easy, Intermediate, & Advanced. Each book contains snare drum etudes written for each of the 40 Rudiments. As a prelude to each etude, there are warm-ups dedicated to the development and mastering of the rudiment it precedes. The overall idea is to have both a technical (the warm-ups) and a musical (the etudes) approach to each of the rudiments. The end result should be not only a mastering of each rudiment, but an applied musicality most often ignored when playing or practicing the rudiments for rudiment's sake.

All of these warm-ups and etudes can also be found on SmartMusic. If you are not familiar with this program, we highly suggest you take a look into it at www.smartmusic.com. The educational advantages presented by SmartMusic are truly incredible, and we are honored to have our books as some of their first percussion pieces. As a bonus feature on SmartMusic, you can find various videos of all these warm-ups and etudes performed by Kit himself.

If you are not familiar with Sandy Feldstein, other than what you have read in this Preface, I encourage you to research his legacy on the web. The more you dig, the more you will be amazed. For the rest of my life, I will be indebted to him. He gave me so many opportunities and always encouraged me to pursue what has made me so much of what I am today. He is missed beyond verbal expression but lives forever in the hearts and deeds of all those he touched in his much too short, yet beautiful, life.

It is in Sandy's memory that we, the authors, hope you find years of enjoyment in using these books for yourself and your students.

Sincerely,
Joe Testa

ABOUT THE AUTHORS:

Kit Chatham is an internationally recognized percussionist, performer, recording artist, arranger, and educator. Kit's experience in many forms of percussion, including drum set, world percussion, orchestral percussion, and marching percussion, makes him a highly sought after performer & clinician and allows him to create a sound uniquely his own.

Kit currently resides in Las Vegas, Nevada, where he is the percussionist for Cirque du Soleil's production, *Viva ELVIS*. Kit has enjoyed performing on stages around the world. Before joining *Viva ELVIS*, he was the percussionist/drummer for Cirque du Soleil's touring show, *Corteo*, which travelled all over North America and Japan; was the featured percussionist for *CyberJam* performing in London's West End; and was the featured snare soloist/percussionist for the Tony and Emmy Award winning Broadway show, *BLAST!*.

Kit has arranged, composed, designed, and instructed for some of the Nation's top music ensembles. This list includes such groups as the Crossmen Drum & Bugle Corp, The University of Georgia, Terminus Percussion Theatre, Atlanta Quest, Odyssey Percussion Theater, and numerous scholastic groups throughout North America.

Kit received his Bachelor's Degree in Music Education from The University of Georgia where he studied with Dr. Thomas McCutchen and Dr. Arvin Scott. While attending, he instructed and arranged for the 2000 Sudler Trophy winning University of Georgia Redcoat Band, performed in numerous ensembles, and toured Europe performing at many prestigious jazz festivals.

Kit continues to give clinics and master classes on percussion around the world and is a proud endorser of Vic Firth Sticks & Mallets, Yamaha Drums & Percussion, Sabian Cymbals, Evans Drumheads, Alternate Mode, and fXpansion Music Software. See more about Kit at *www.KitChatham.com*.

Steve Murphy, for the past 18 years, has been the band director at Onteora Middle/High School in Boiceville, NY. Steve serves as percussion caption head for the Kingston High School Marching Band in Kingston, NY, as well as the director of the Onteora Jazz Ensemble, the Onteora Marching Band, and the Onteora Percussion Ensemble. Under his direction, the Onteora Middle School Band has received numerous Gold and Silver ratings at NYSSMA Major Ensemble festivals; and the Onteora Marching Band is a former Musical Arts Conference "Class II" Champion and has earned several 1st Place awards at the annual New York City St. Patrick's Day Parade.

Steve received his Bachelor's of Music Education and Master's in Percussion Performance from the Crane School of Music at SUNY Potsdam where he studied with James Petercsak. Steve is also a member of MENC, the New York State School Music Association, the Percussive Arts Society, and the Ulster County Music Educators Association.

Joe Testa is highly respected in the music industry and began his career after earning a Bachelor of Music from the Crane School of Music at SUNY Potsdam, New York. He first put his knowledge into action working for Warner Bros Publications in Miami, Florida, under the tutelage of his mentor Sandy Feldstein. It was during this time Joe became an accomplished editor, author, businessman, and leader himself. He produced, coordinated and authored best-selling instructional media with high-profile artists including Russ Miller, Gavin Harrison, and Akira Jimbo and respected educators such as Steve Houghton. Additionally, Joe orchestrated the creation of numerous instructional music publications and videos.

Joe moved to California when he became international artist relations manager for Yamaha Corporation of America. He was an extremely successful corporate event producer of annual Groove Night and Groove All Stars drum events, which included special appearances by Michael McDonald, Jackson Browne, and Ellis Hall and were held in the US, Mexico and Germany. He proudly found himself working alongside celebrated drummers such as Rick Marotta, Steve Jordan, Carter Beauford, Manu Katche, Keith Carlock, and his own drum hero, Steve Gadd.

As a freelance producer, editor, writer, and consultant for publishing and visual marketing projects, Joe was the director and producer of Memphis Drum Shop's *Cymbal Summit 2010 Weekend* and of Mapex's Falcon promotional *Let Your Feet Fly* video. One of his most rewarding roles was as writer and video producer of MakeMusic Inc.'s Rudimental Project, which was SmartMusic's debut of online percussion material—a treasured project given to him by Sandy. Other clients include Sabian, Dreamland Recording Studios, Carl Fischer Music, and Warner Bros Publications.

Currently, Joe can be found in Massachusetts as director of artist relations for Vic Firth Company. There, he oversees the talent of over 2900 artists, including Cindy Blackman, Matt Cameron, Abe Laboriel Jr., and Charlie Watts. Joe is actively preparing, monitoring, and developing global projects and promotions including signature product contracts, artist signings, video production, educational tours, recording, film, tours, performances, and endorsements.

ABOUT SMARTMUSIC:

Cool tools for drumming at home!

SmartMusic is award-winning interactive music software that provides the ideal practice environment.

Practice all the études in this book with SmartMusic:
- Listen to performances by professional percussionists and hear how they interpret the written part.
- Slow the tempo or repeat difficult sections.
- Record and listen to your performance.
- Incorporate a click track.
- Use the optional cursor as a visual reference while you are learning new rhythms.

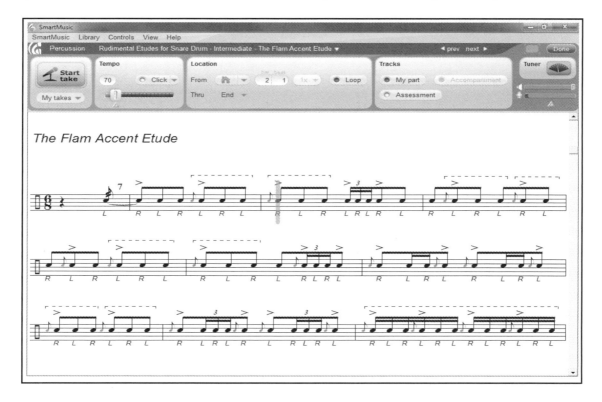

Explore the repertoire
SmartMusic has a lot of songs for you to practice along with:
- more than 2,700 titles for concert band, jazz ensemble, or string and full orchestra
- jazz repertoire and innovative tools for learning and practicing improvisation

Getting started is easy. Visit www.smartmusic.com or call 866.240.4041

THE ROLL RUDIMENTS:

Rudiment is included in the Original 26

I. SINGLE STROKE ROLL RUDIMENTS

SINGLE STROKE ROLL*

SINGLE STROKE 4

SINGLE STROKE 7

II. MULTIPLE BOUNCE ROLL RUDIMENTS

MULTIPLE BOUNCE ROLL

TRIPLE STROKE ROLL

III. DOUBLE STROKE OPEN ROLL RUDIMENTS

DOUBLE STROKE OPEN ROLL*

10 STROKE ROLL*

5 STROKE ROLL*

11 STROKE ROLL*

6 STROKE ROLL

13 STROKE ROLL*

7 STROKE ROLL*

15 STROKE ROLL*

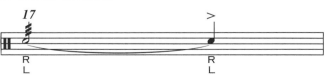

9 STROKE ROLL*

17 STROKE ROLL

The Single Stroke Roll

Rudiment Included in the Original 26

Also Written As:

Single Stroke Roll Warm-Ups:

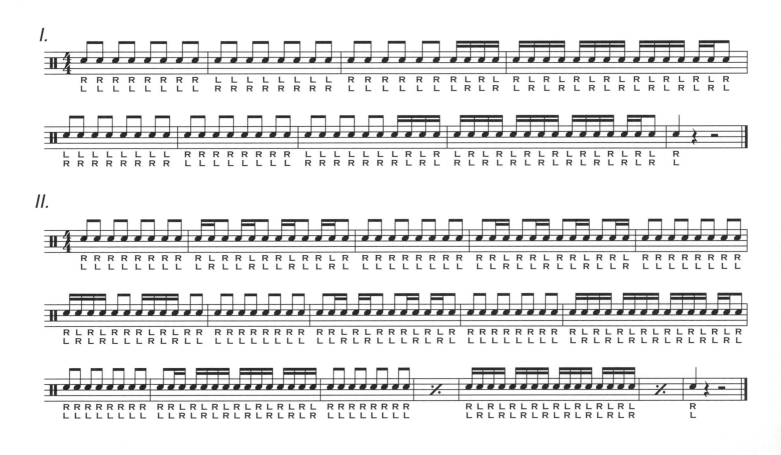

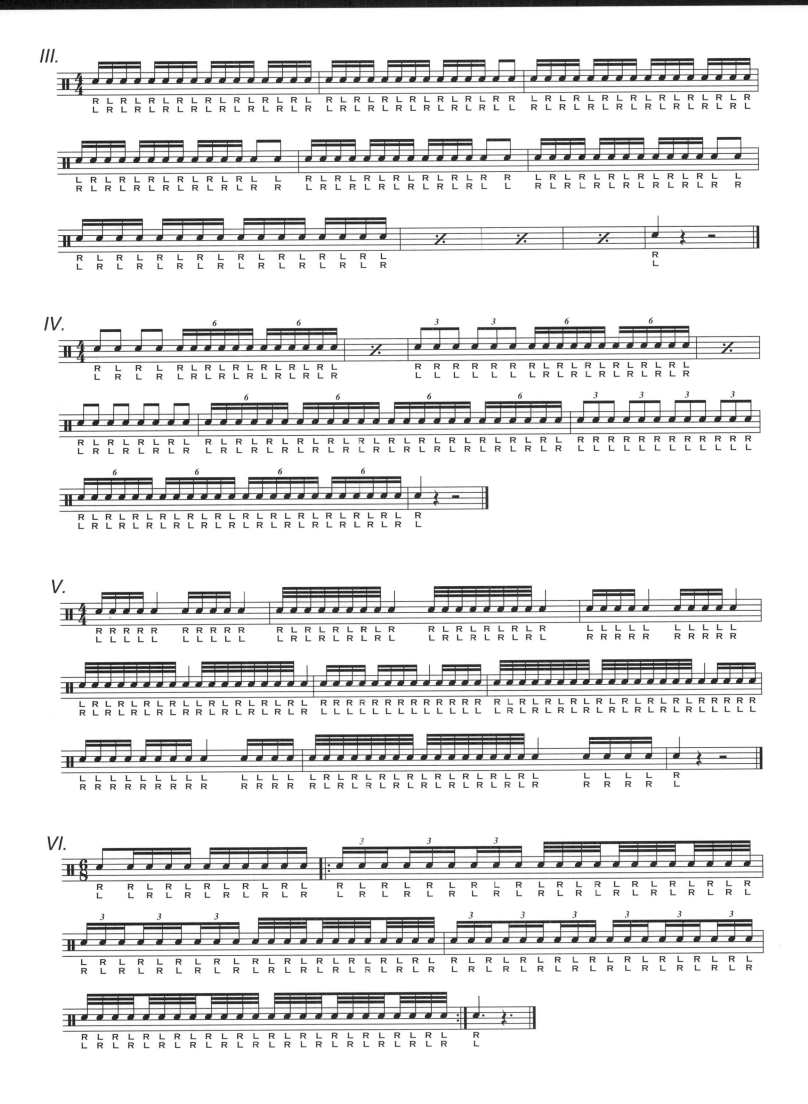

The Single Stroke Roll Etude
- perform etude at various tempos and dynamics

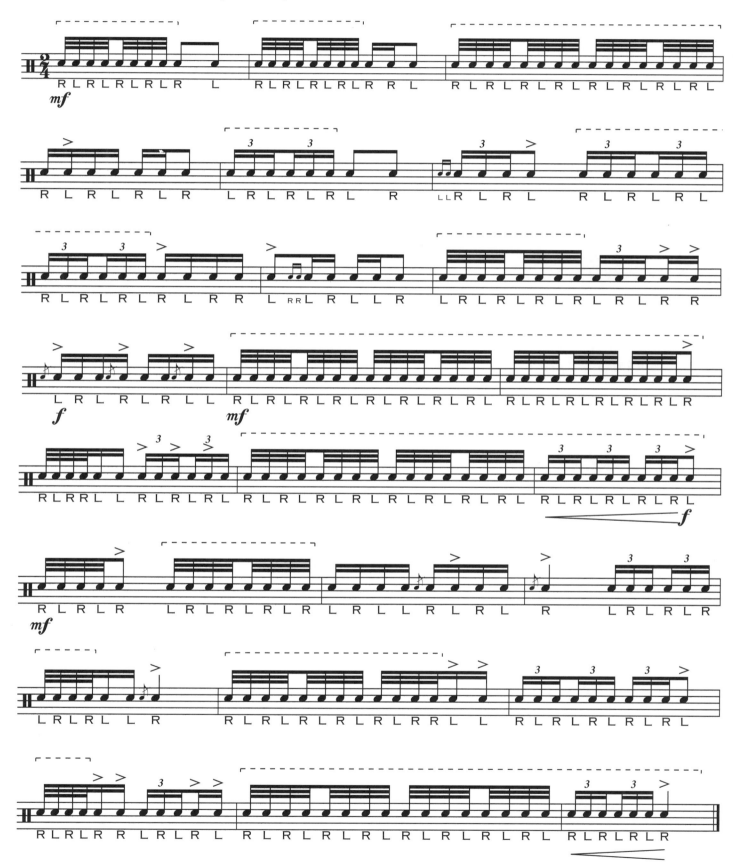

The Single Stroke 4

Also Written As:

Single Stroke 4 Warm-Ups:

The Single Stroke 4 Etude

- perform etude at various tempos and dynamics

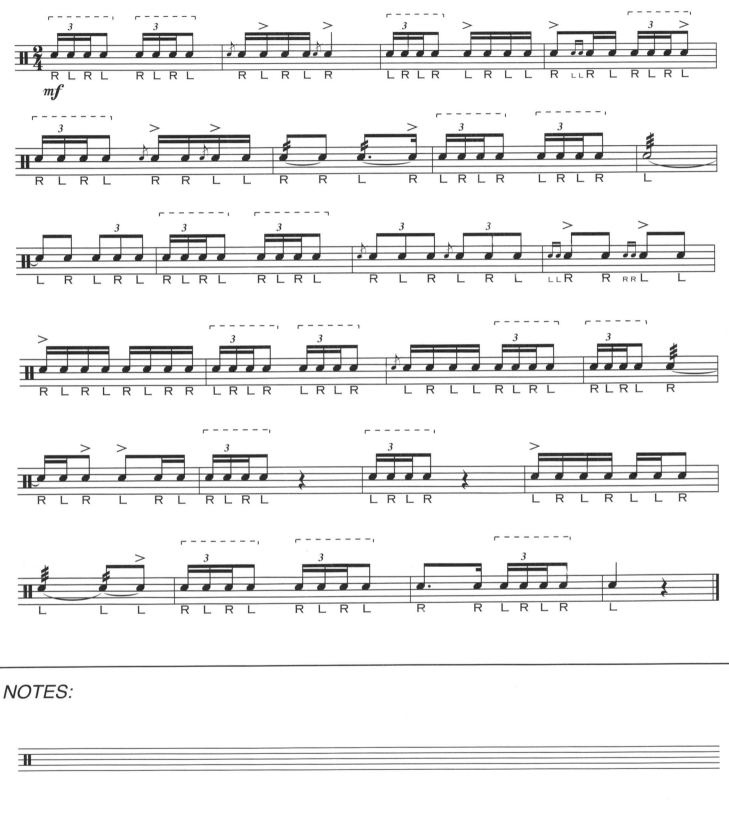

The Single Stroke 7

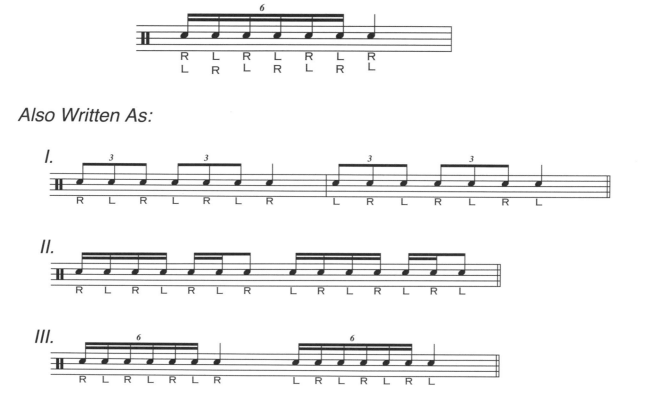

Also Written As:

Single Stroke 7 Warm-Ups:

The Single Stoke 7 Etude
- *perform etude at various tempos and dynamics*

The Multiple Bounce Roll

Also Written As:

Multiple Bounce Roll Warm-Ups:

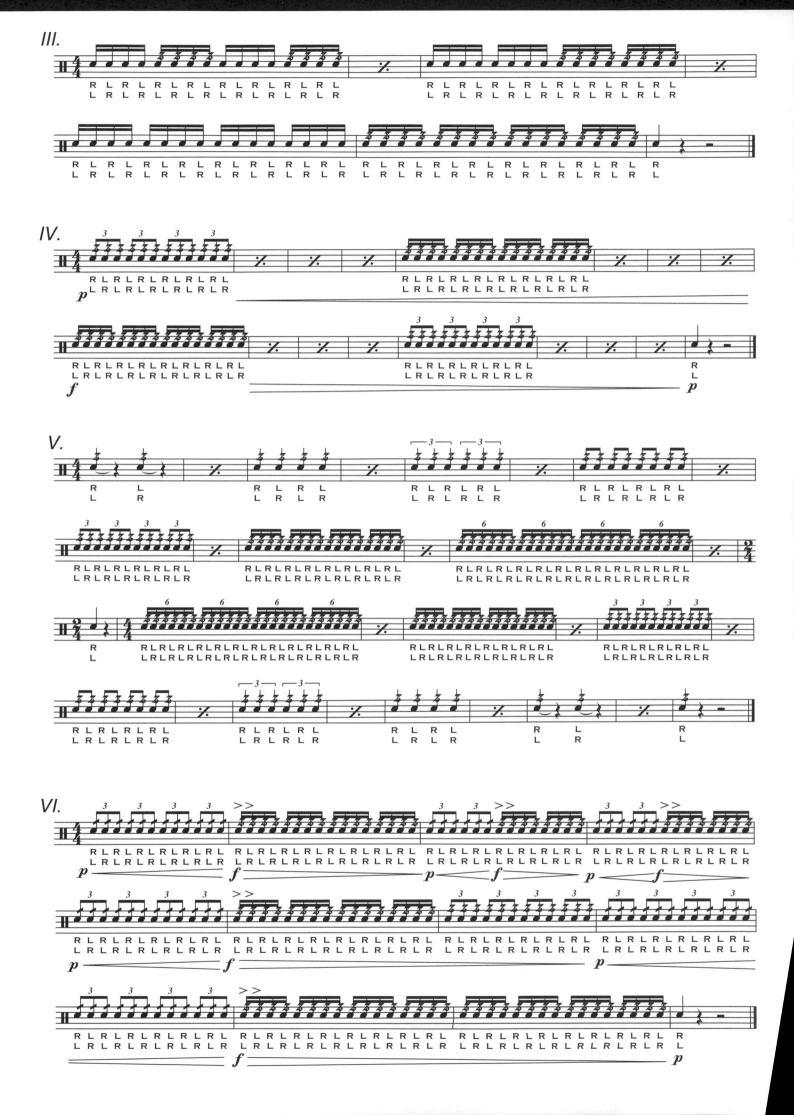

The Mutliple Bounce Roll Etude

- perform etude at various tempos and dynamics

The Triple Stroke Roll

R R R L L L R R R L L L

Also Written As:

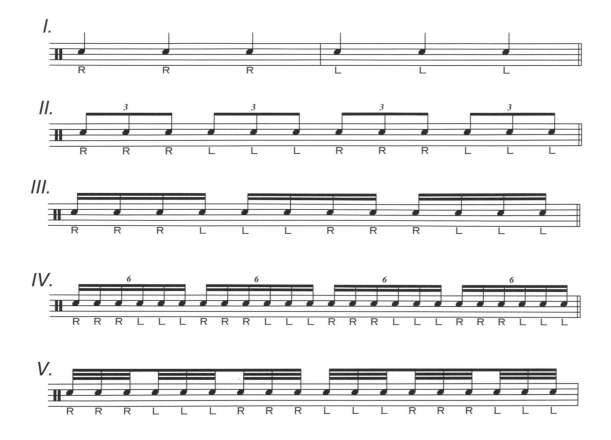

Triple Stroke Roll Warm-Ups:

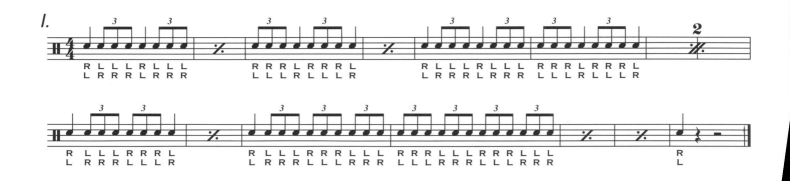

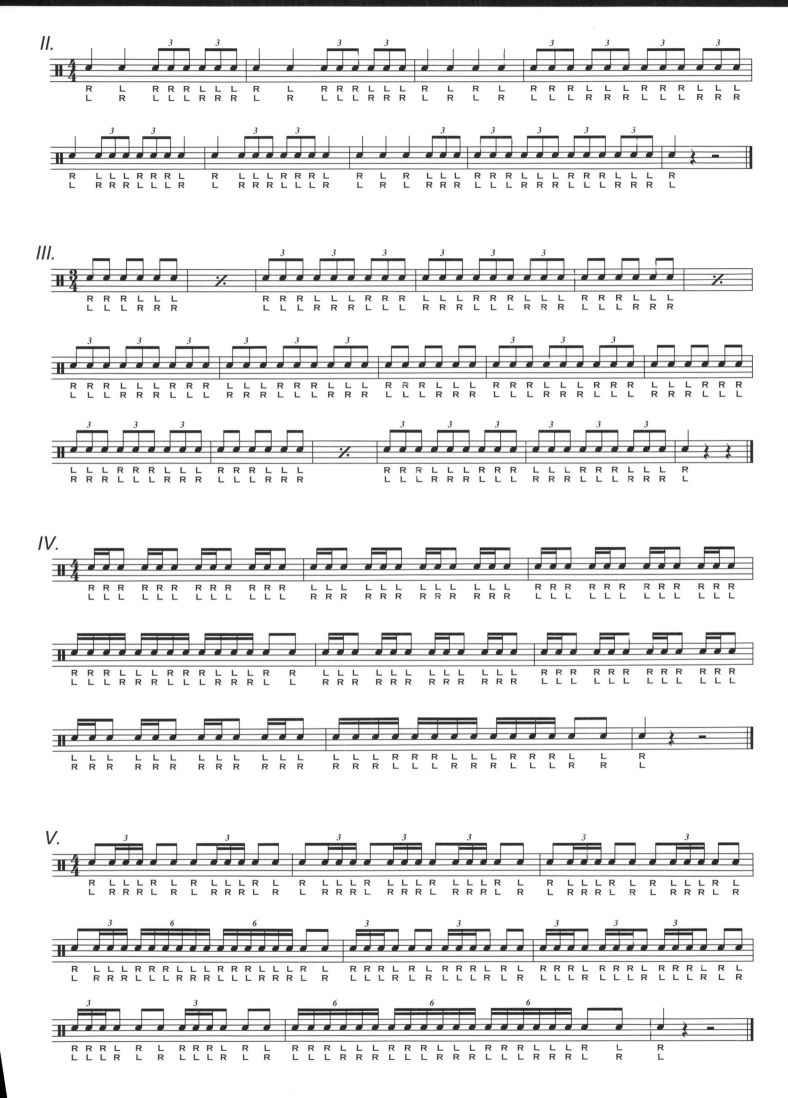

The Triple Stroke Roll Etude
- perform etude at various tempos and dynamics

The Double Stroke Roll (Long Roll)
Rudiment Included in the Original 26

RRLLRRLLRRLLRRLL

Also Written As:

Double Stroke Roll Warm-Ups:

The Double Stroke Roll Etude
- perform etude at various tempos and dynamics

The 5 Stroke Roll
Rudiment Included in the Original 26

Also Written As:

On the Beat Version   The Off-Beat Version

5 Stroke Roll Warm-Ups:

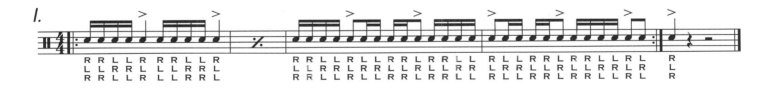

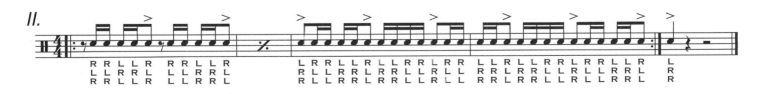

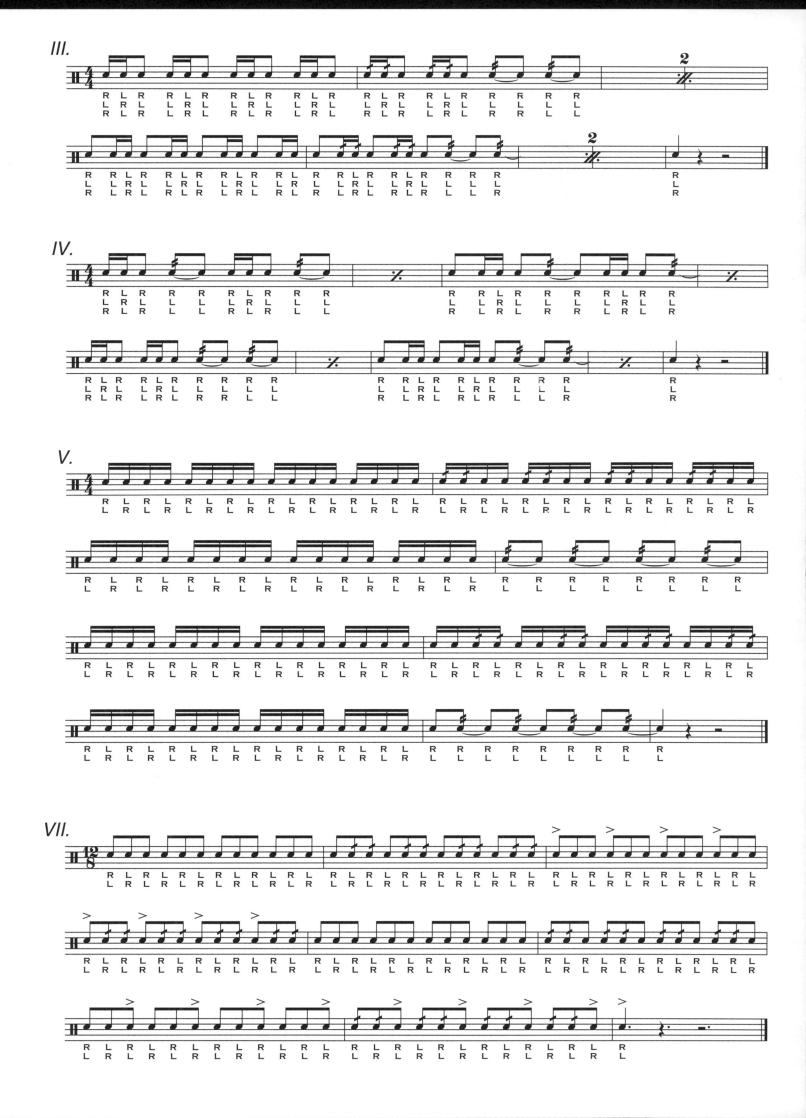

The 5 Stroke Roll Etude
- perform etude at various tempos and dynamics

The 6 Stroke Roll

Also Written As:

I.

II.

III.

IV.

V.

6 Stroke Roll Warm-Ups:

I.

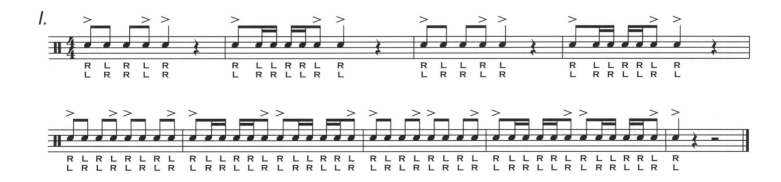

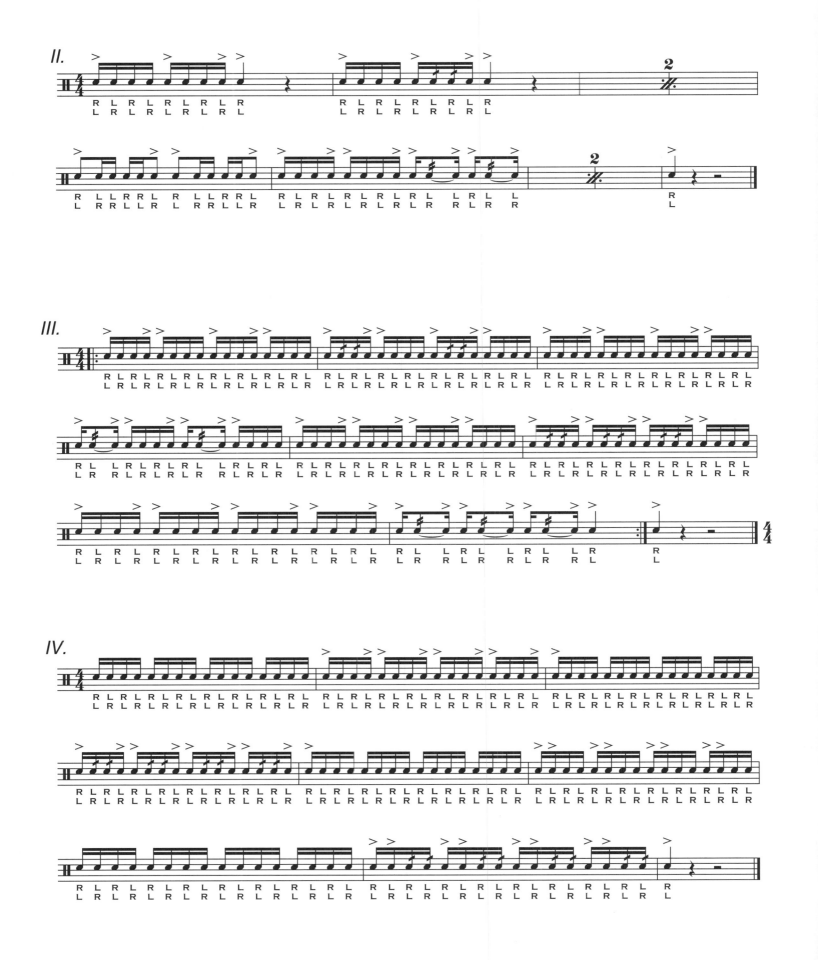

The 6 Stroke Roll Etude
- perform etude at various tempos and dynamics

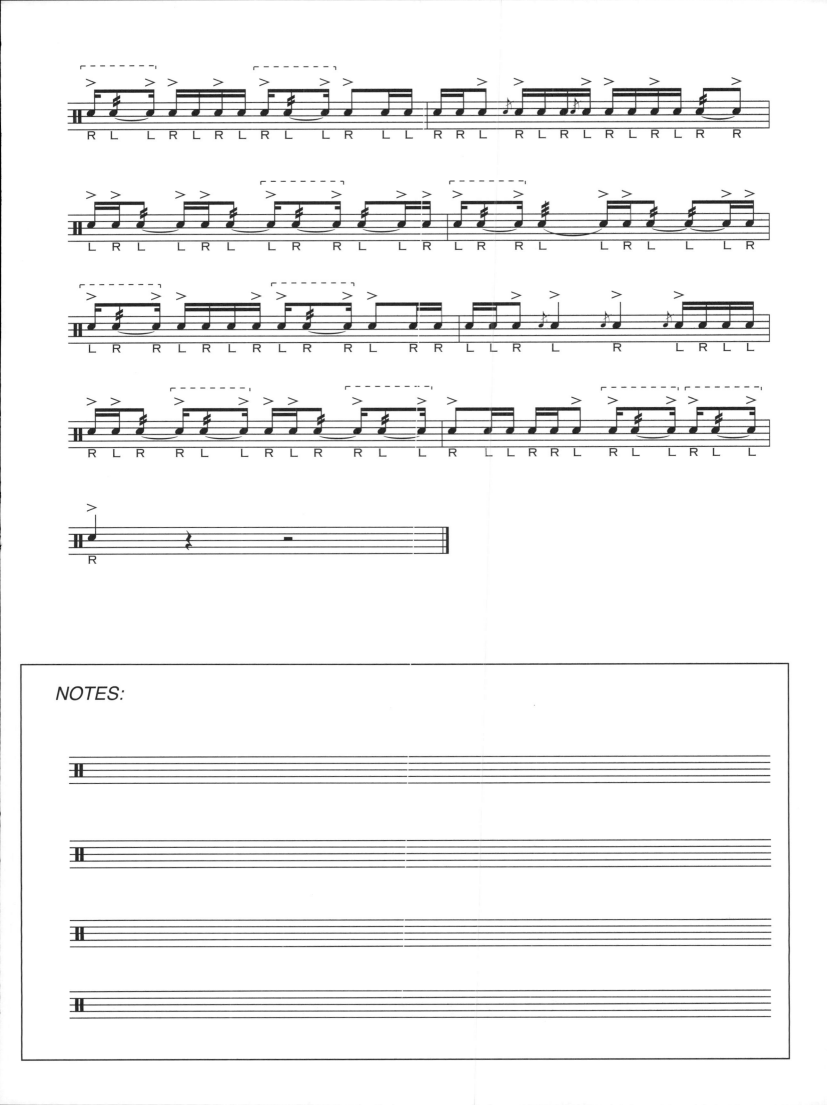

NOTES:

The 7 Stroke Roll
Rudiment Included in the Original 26

Also Written As:

On The Beat Version   The Off-Beat Version

7 Stroke Warm-Ups:

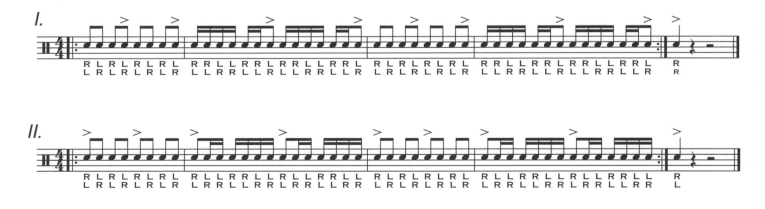

The 7 Stroke Roll Etude
- perform etude at various tempos and dynamics

The 9 Stroke Roll
Rudiment Included in the Original 26

Also Written As:

9 Stroke Roll Warm-Ups:

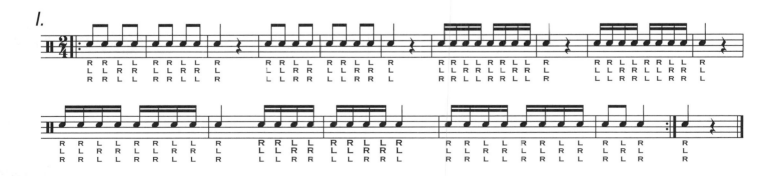

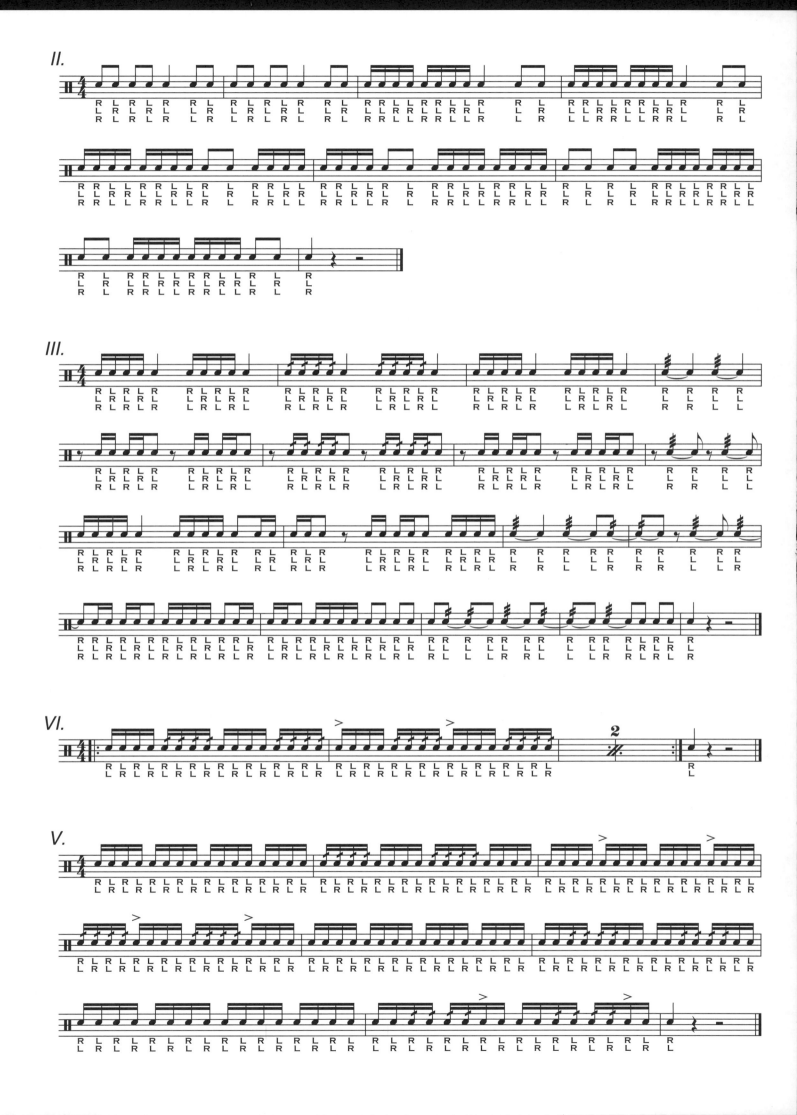

The 9 Stroke Roll Etude
- *perform etude at various tempos and dynamics*

The 10 Stroke Roll
*Rudiment Included in the Original 26

Also Written As:

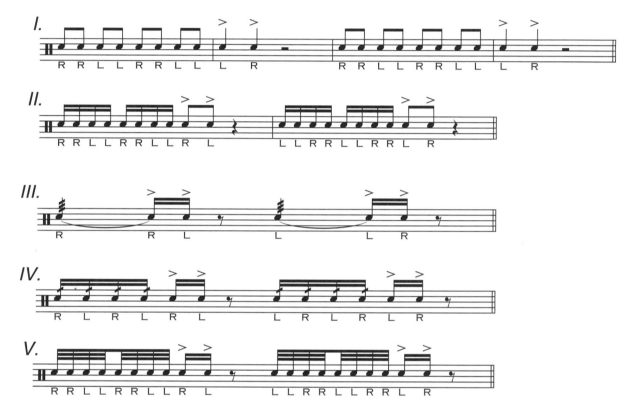

10 Stroke Roll Warm-Ups:

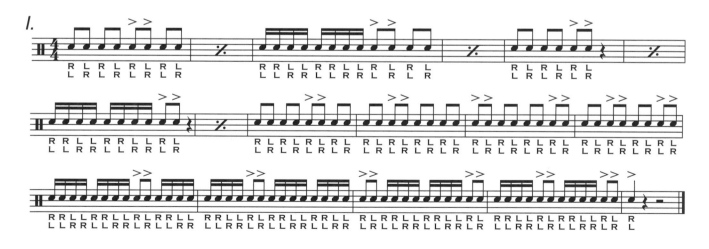

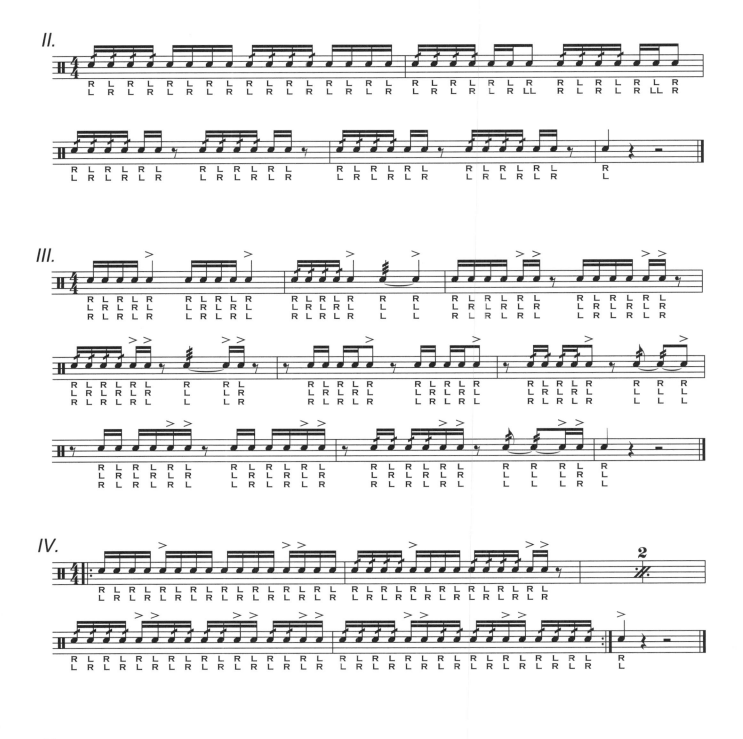

The 10 Stroke Roll Etude
- perform etude at various tempos and dynamics

The 11 Stroke Roll
Rudiment Included in the Original 26

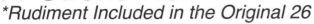

Also Written As:

11 Stroke Roll Warm-Ups:

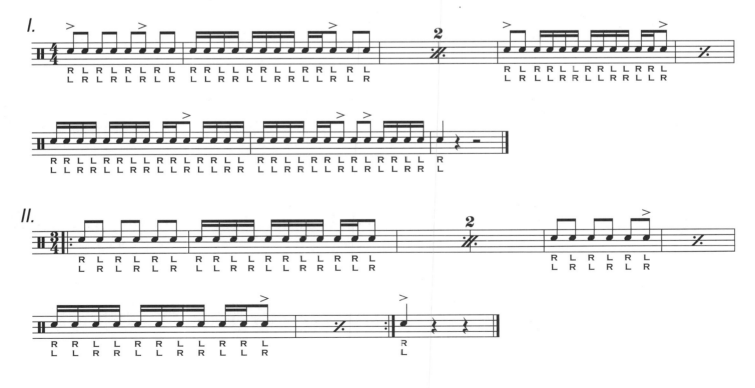

The 11 Stroke Roll Etude

- perform etude at various tempos and dynamics

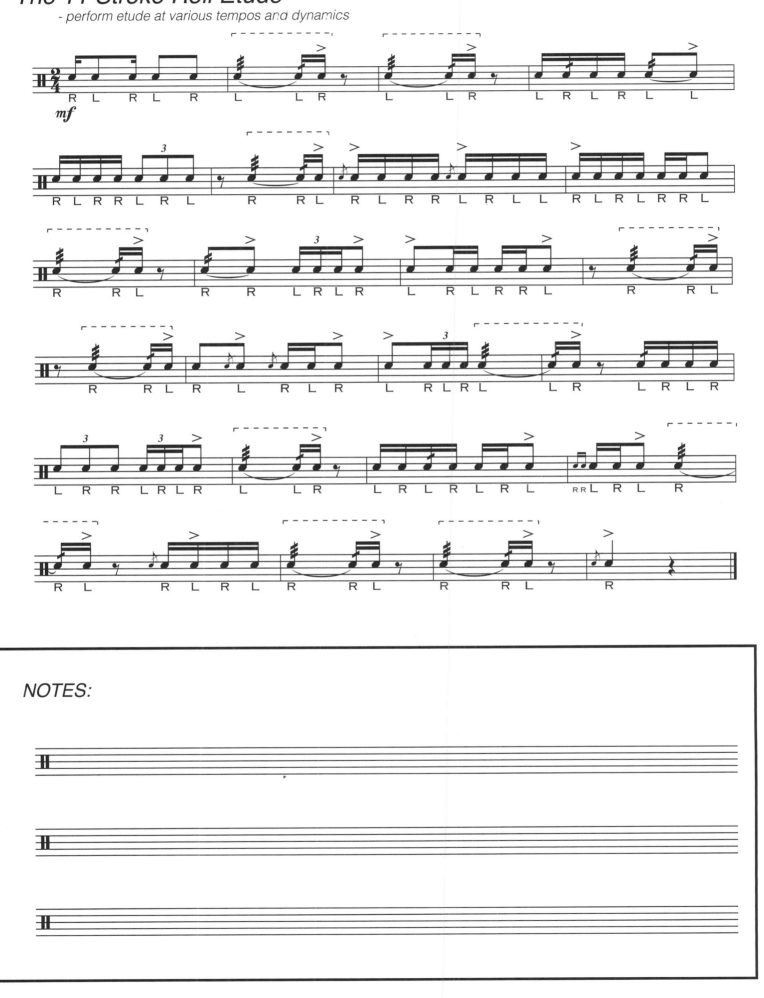

NOTES:

The 13 Stroke Roll
*Rudiment Included in the Original 26

Also Written As:

13 Stroke Roll Warm-Ups:

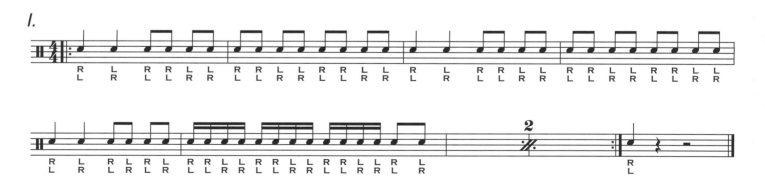

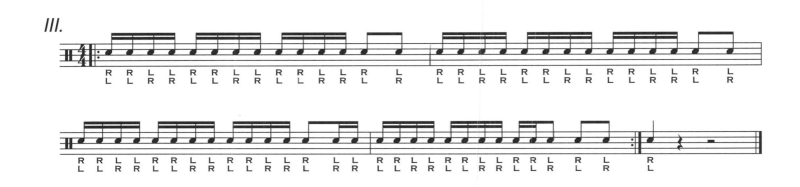

The 13 Stroke Roll Etude
- perform etude at various tempos and dynamics

The 15 Stroke Roll
*Rudiment Included in the Original 26

Also Written As:

On The Beat Version	The Off-Beat Version

I.

II.

III.

IV.

V.

15 Stroke Roll Warm-Ups:

I.

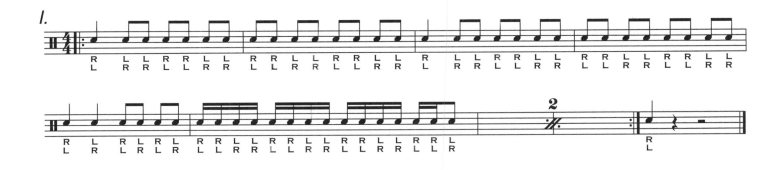

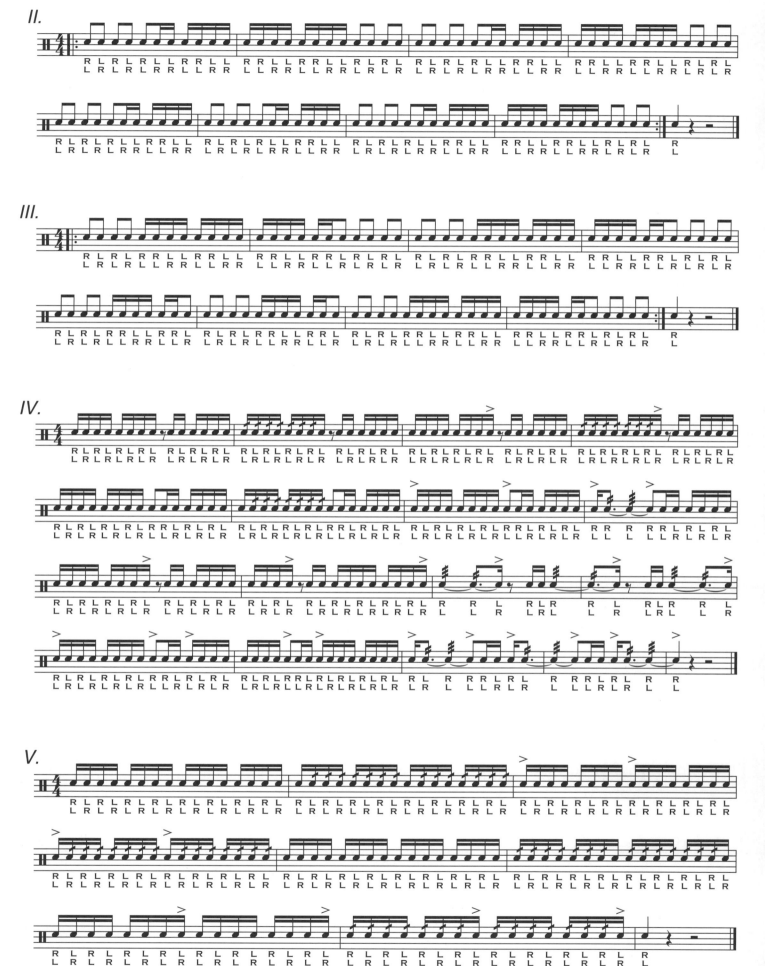

The 15 Stroke Roll Etude

- perform etude at various tempos and dynamics

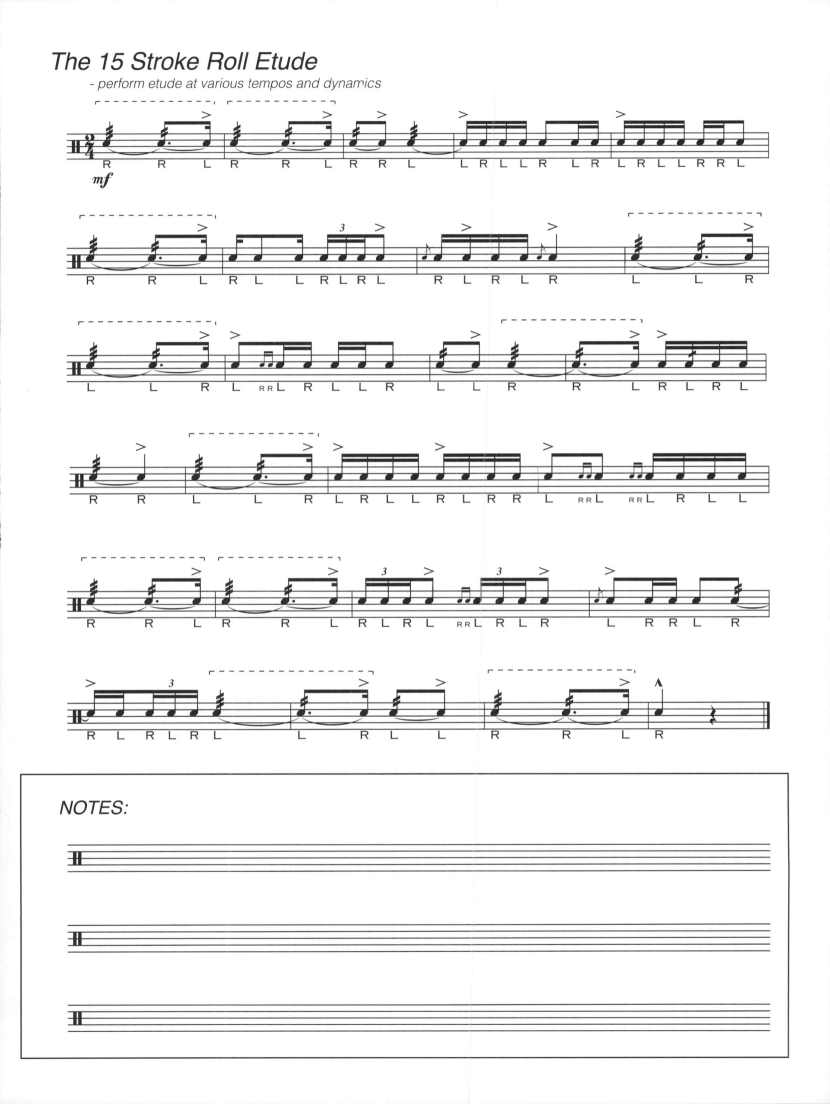

The 17 Stroke Roll

Also Written As:

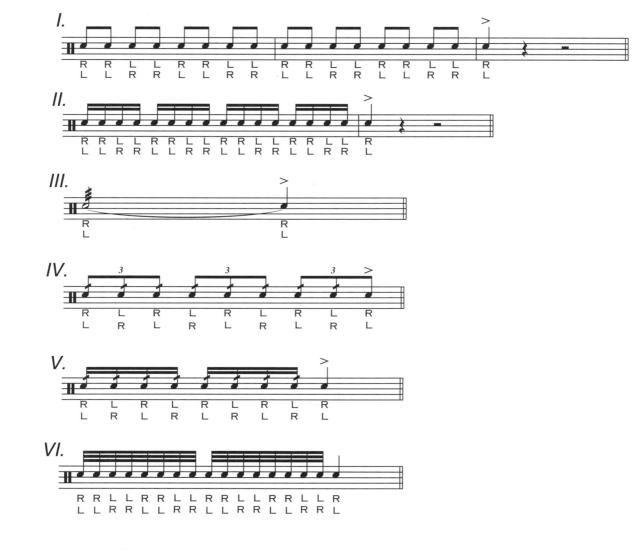

17 Stroke Roll Warm-Ups:

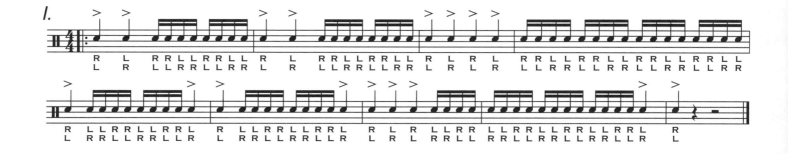

II.

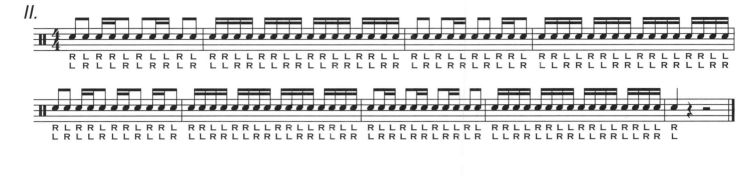

RLRRLRLLRL   RRLLRRLLRRLLRLL   RLRLLLRLRRL   RRLLRRLLRRLLRRLL
LRLLLRLRRLR   LLRRLLRRLLRRLLRR   LRLRRLRLLLR   LLRRLLRRLLRRLLRR

RLRRLRRLRRL   RRLLRRLLRRLLRLL   RLLRLLRLLRL   RRLLRRLLRRLLRLL   R
LRLLLRLLLRL   LRRLLRRLLRRLLRR   LRRLRRLRRLR   LLRRLLRRLLRRLLRR   L

III.

RLRLLLRRLRLL   RRLLRRLLRRLLRRL   RRLRLLRRLLRRLL   RRLLRRLRLLLRRL
LLRLRRLLRLRR   LLRRLLRRLLRRLLR   LLRLRRLLRRLLRR   LLRRLLRLRRRLLR

RLLRRLLRRLLRRLL   RRLRLLRRLRL   RRLLRRLLRRLLRRLL   RLLRRLLRRLLRRLL   RRLRL
LRRLLRRLLRRLLRR   LLRLRRLLRLR   LLRRLLRRLLRRLLRR   LRRLLRRLLRRLLRR   LLRLR

IV.

RLRLRLRLRLRLRLRL   RLRLRLRLRLRLRLRL   RLRLRLRLRLR   RLRLRLRLR   R
LRLRLRLRLRLRLRLR   LRLRLRLRLRLRLRLR   LRLRLRLRLRL   LRLRLRLRL   L

V.

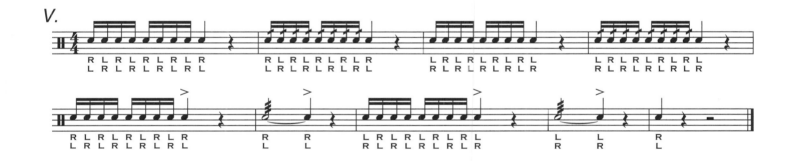

RLRLRLRLR   RLRLRLRLR   LRLRLRLRL   LRLRLRLRL
LRLRLRLRL   LRLRLRLRL   RLRLRLRLR   RLRLRLRLR

RLRLRLRLR   R   R   LRLRLRLRL   L   L   R
LRLRLRLRL   L   L   RLRLRLRLR   R   R   L

VI.

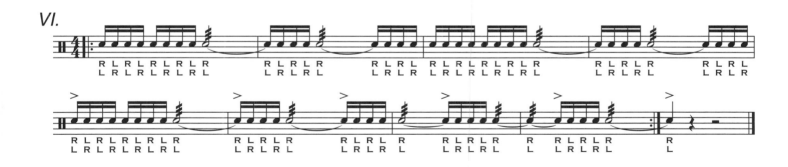

RLRLRLRLR   RLRLR   RLRL   RLRLRLRLR   RLRLR   RLRL
LRLRLRLRL   LRLRL   LRLR   LRLRLRLRL   LRLRL   LRLR

RLRLRLRLR   RLRLR   RLRL   R   RLRLR   R   RLRLR   R
LRLRLRLRL   LRLRL   LRLR   L   LRLRL   L   LRLRL   L

VII.

RLRLRLRLR   RLRLRLRLR   R   R   RL   RLRLRLR   RLRL   RLRLR   R   R   RL   RLRLRLRL   R   RLRLRLRL
LRLRLRLRL   LRLRLRLRL   L   L   LR   L   L   LR   LRL   LRLR   L   L   LR   LRLRLRLR   L   LRLRLRLR

R   RLRLRLRL   RLR   R   R   RLRLRLRL   RLRLRLR   RLR   RLRL   RLRLRLRL   R   R   RL   RLRLRLRL   R
L   LRLRLRLR   LRL   L   L   LRLRLRLR   LRLRLRL   LRL   LRLR   LRLRLRLR   L   L   LR   LRLRLRLR   L

The 17 Stroke Roll Etude
- perform etude at various tempos and dynamics

SECTION 2

THE DIDDLE RUDIMENTS:

Rudiment is included in the Original 26

SINGLE PARADIDDLE*

R L R R L R L L

DOUBLE PARADIDDLE*

R L R L R R L R L R L L

TRIPLE PARADIDDLE

R L R L R L R R L R L R L R L L

SINGLE PARADIDDLE-DIDDLE

R L R R L L R L R R L L
L R L L R R L R L L R R

The Single Paradiddle
Rudiment Included in the Original 26

Also Written As:

Single Paradiddle Warm-Ups:

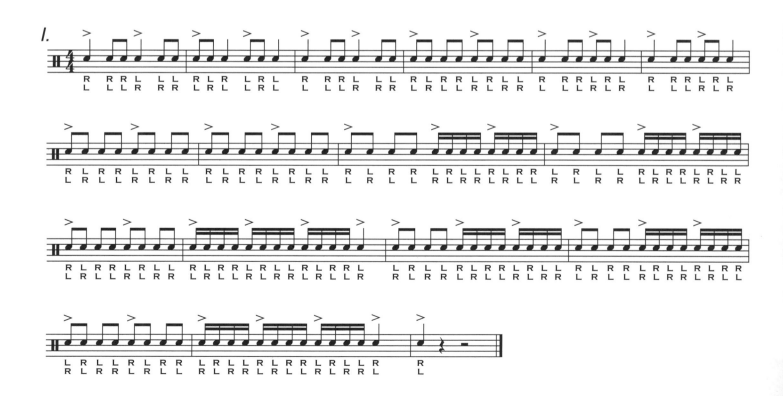

The Single Paradiddle Etude
- perform etude at various tempos and dynamics

NOTES:

The Double Paradiddle
*Rudiment Included in the Original 26

Also Written As:

Double Paradiddle Warm-Ups:

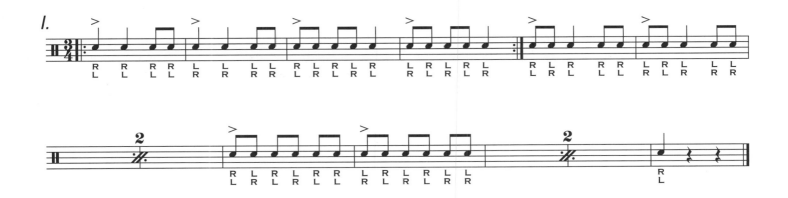

The Double Paradiddle Etude
- *perform etude at various tempos and dynamics*

The Triple Paradiddle

R L R L R L R R L R L R L R L L

Also Written As:

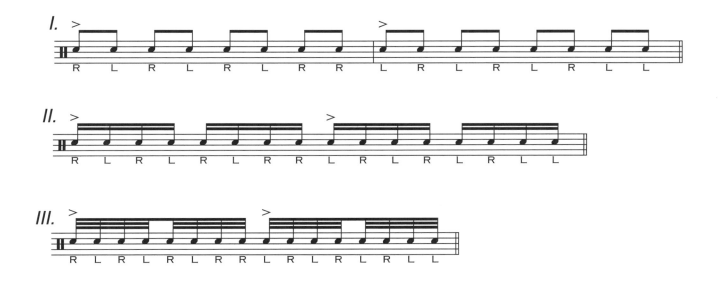

Triple Paradiddle Warm-Ups:

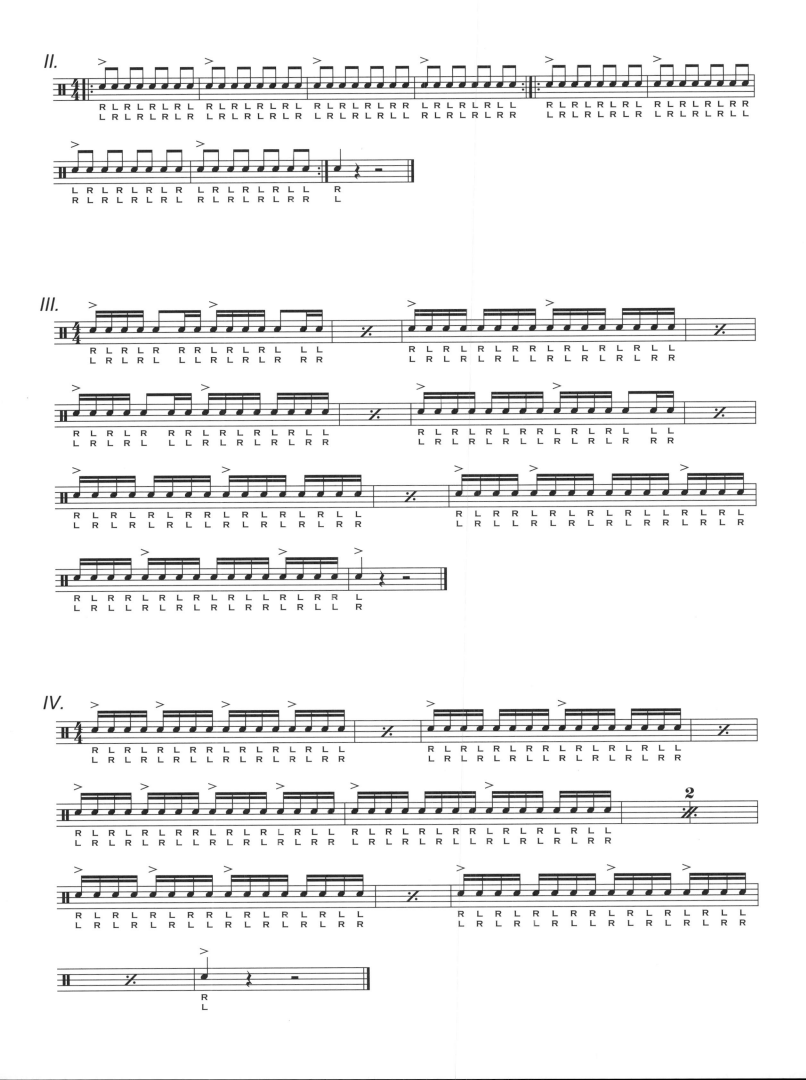

The Triple Paradiddle Etude
- perform etude at various tempos and dynamics

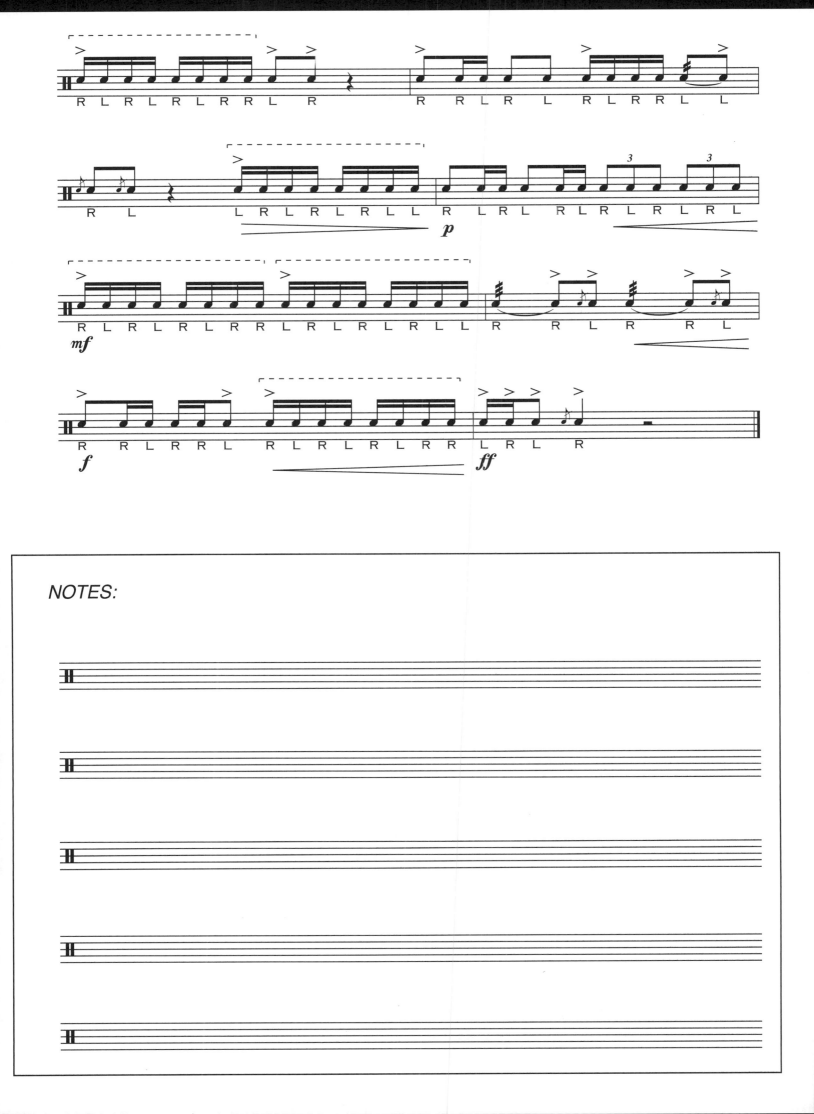

NOTES:

The Single Paradiddle-Diddle

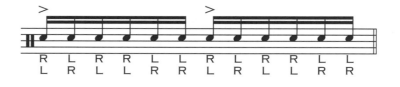

Also Written As:

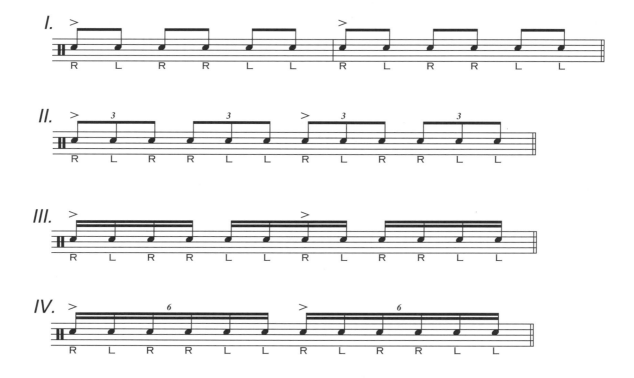

Single Paradiddle-Diddle Warm-Ups:

II.

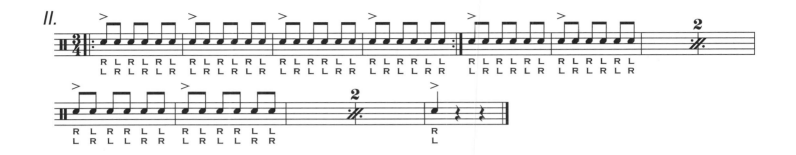

III.

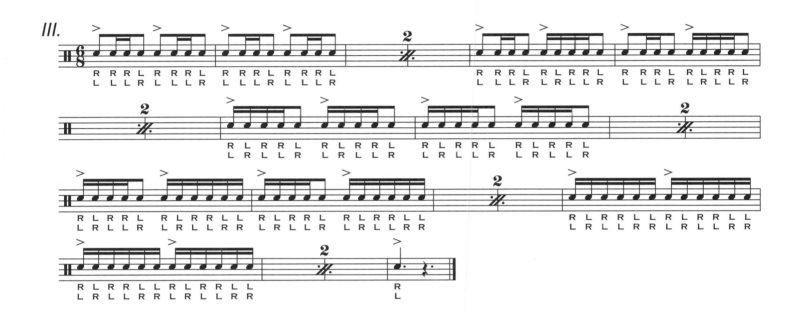

IV.

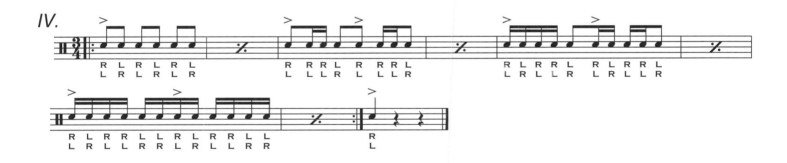

V.

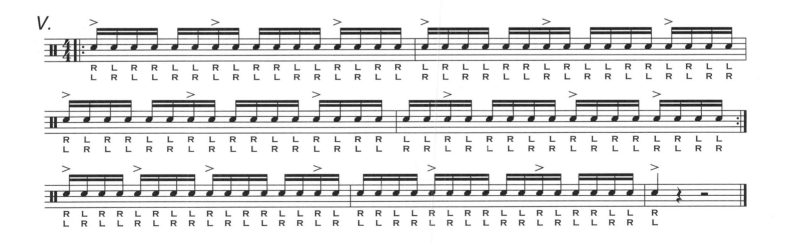

The Single Paradiddle-Diddle Etude

- perform etude at various tempos and dynamics

SECTION 3

THE FLAM RUDIMENTS:

*Rudiment is included in the Original 26

FLAM*

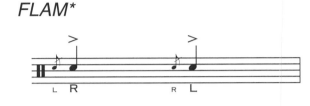

FLAM ACCENT*

FLAM PARADIDDLE-DIDDLE*

FLAM TAP*

PATAFLAFLA

FLAMACUE*

SWISS ARMY TRIPLET

FLAM PARADIDDLE*

INVERTED FLAM TAP

SINGLE FLAMMED MILL

FLAM DRAG

The Flam
*Rudiment Included in the Original 26

Aslo Written As:

I.

II.

Flam Warm-Ups:

The Flam Etude
- perform etude at various tempos and dynamics

The Flam Accent
Rudiment Included in the Original 26

Also Written As:

I.

II.

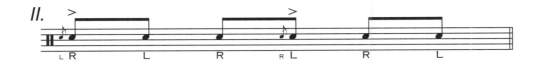

III.

IV.

V.

Flam Accent Warm-Ups:

I.

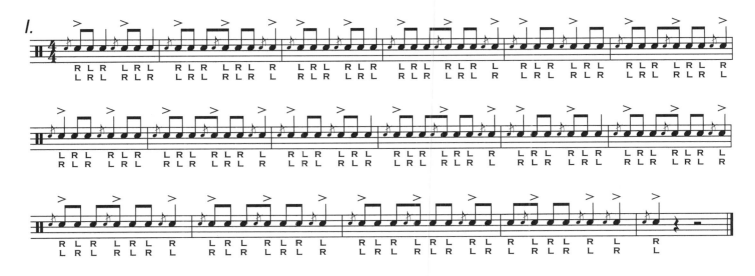

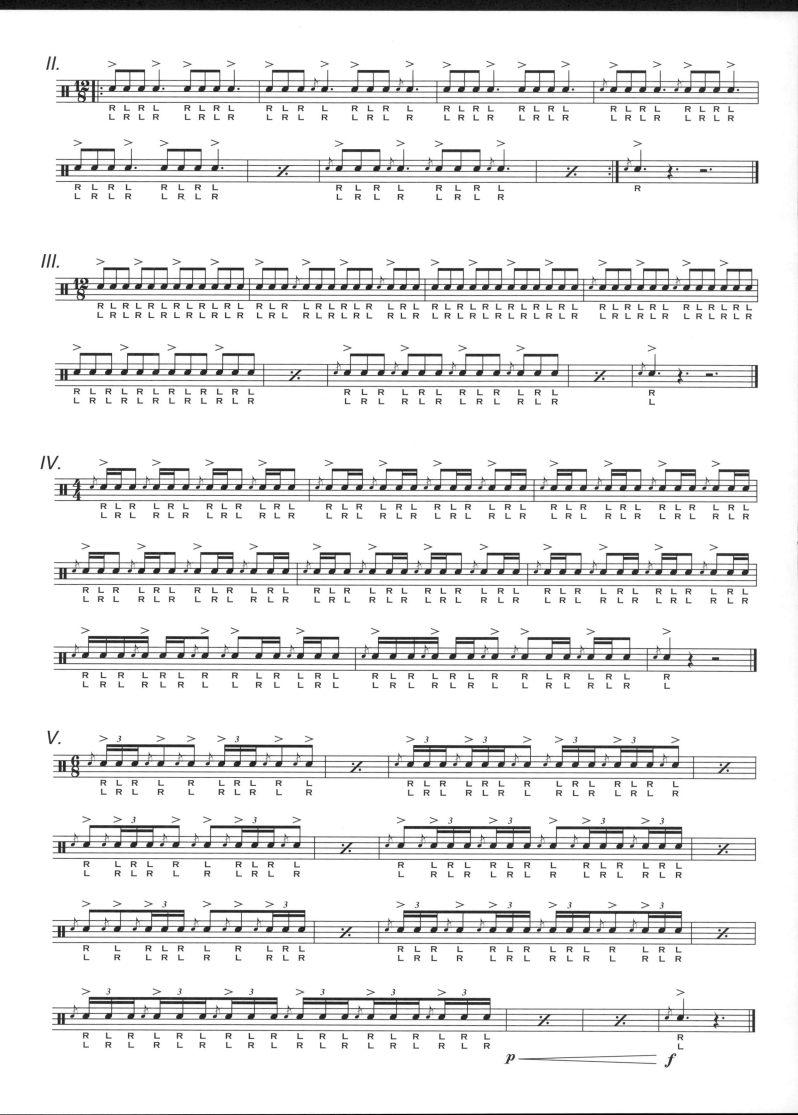

The Flam Accent Etude

- perform etude at various tempos and dynamics

The Flam Tap
Rudiment Included in the Original 26

Also Written As:

Flam Tap Warm-Ups:

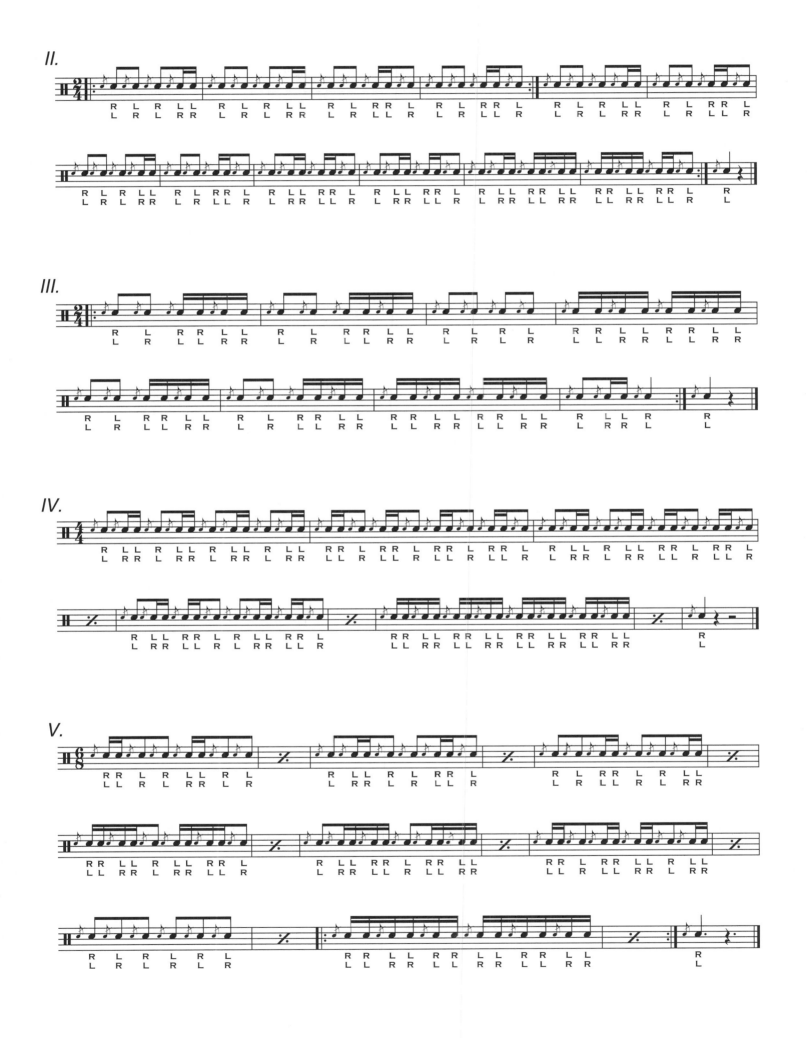

The Flam Tap Etude

- perform etude at various tempos and dynamics

The Flamacue
Rudiment Included in the Original 26

Also Written As:

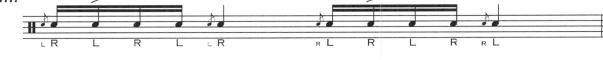

Flamacue Warm-Ups:

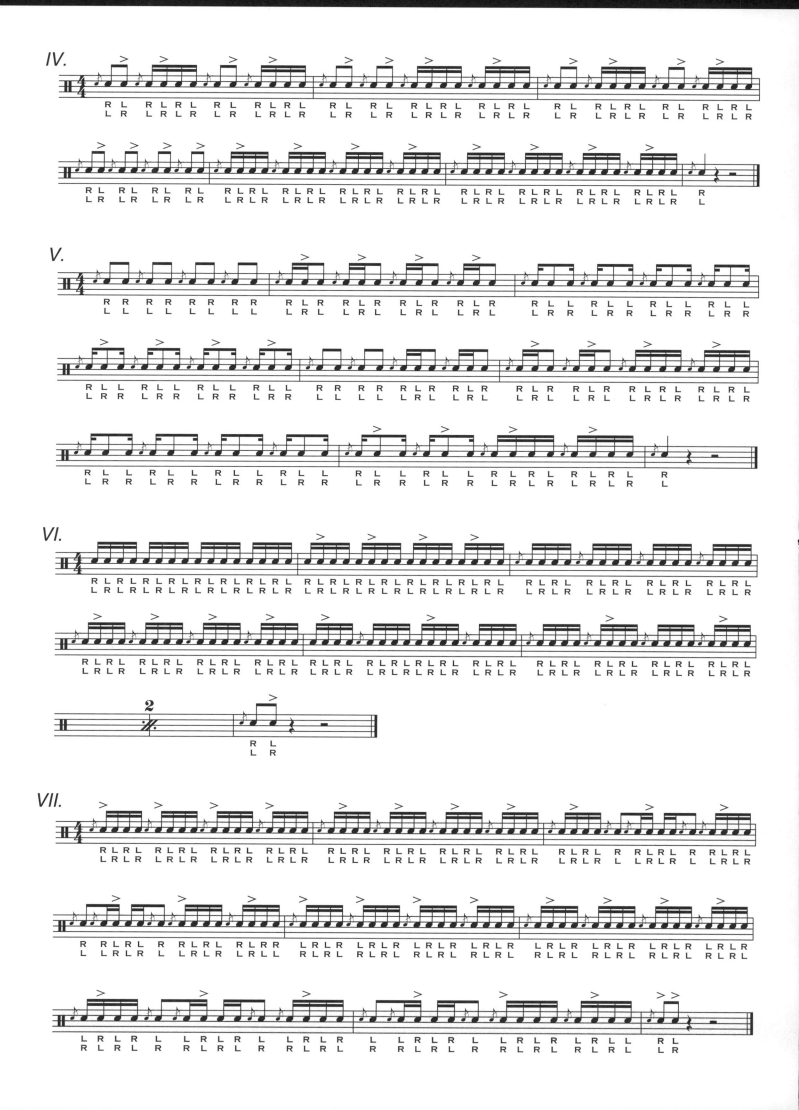

The Flamacue Etude

- perform etude at various tempos and dynamics

The Flam Paradiddle
Rudiment Included in the Original 26

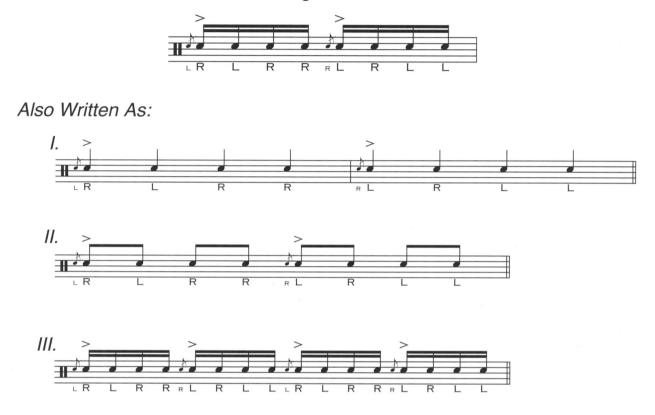

Also Written As:

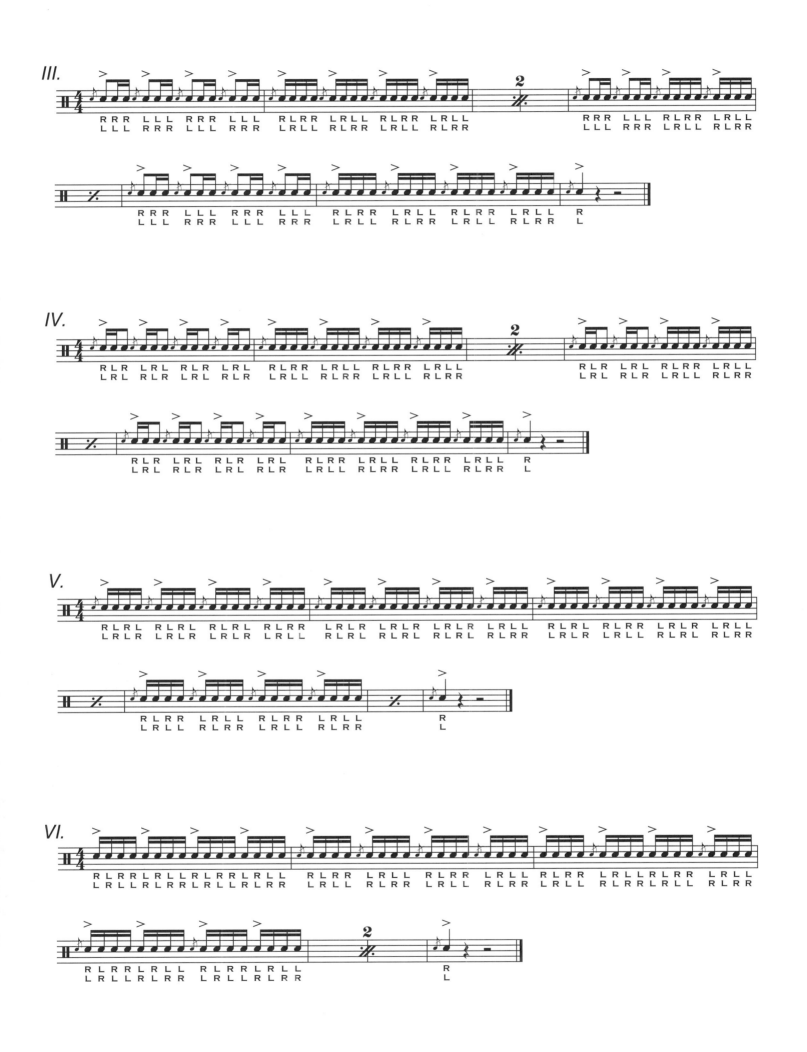

The Flam Paradiddle Etude

- perform etude at various tempos and dynamics

Kit Chatham recording all the etudes in this book
for the SMARTMUSIC Percussion Project

The Single Flammed Mill

Also Written As:

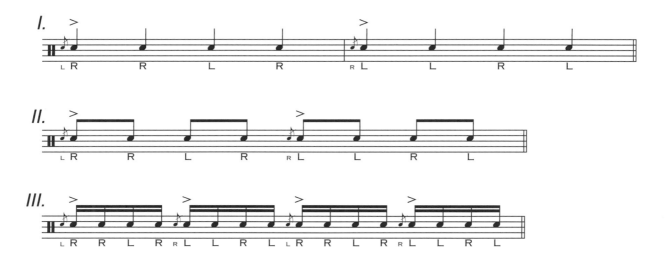

Single Flammed Mill Warm-Ups:

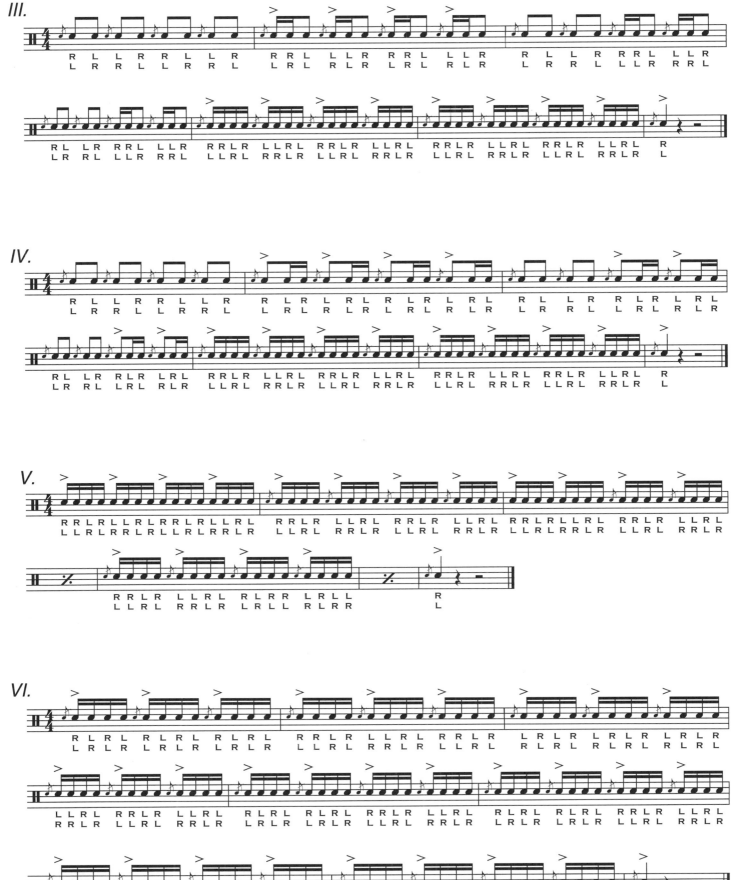

The Single Flammed Mill Etude
- perform etude at various tempos and dynamics

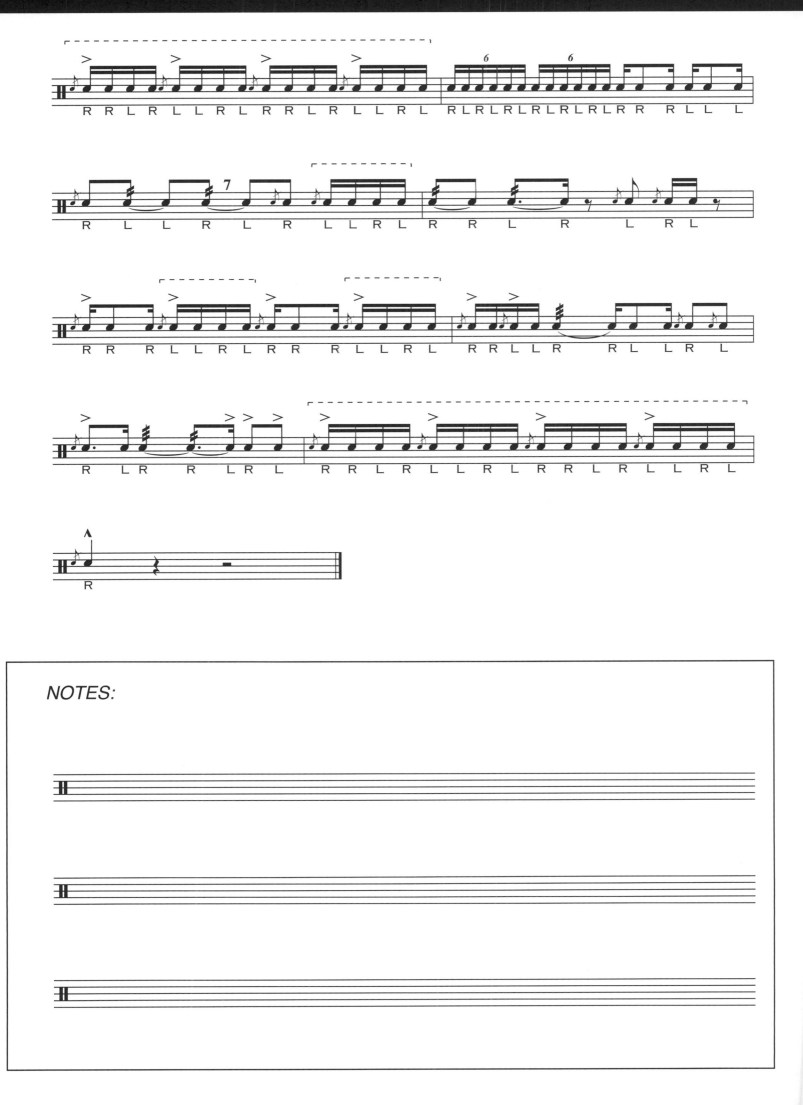

The Flam Paradiddle-Diddle
Rudiment Included in the Original 26

Also Written As:

Flam Paradiddle-Diddle Warm-Ups:

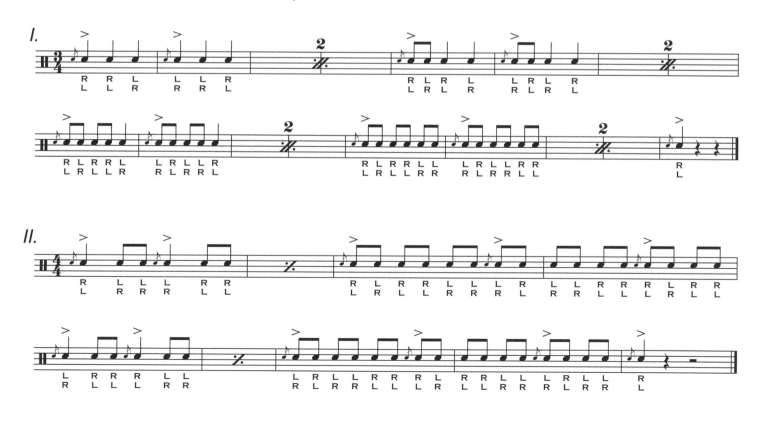

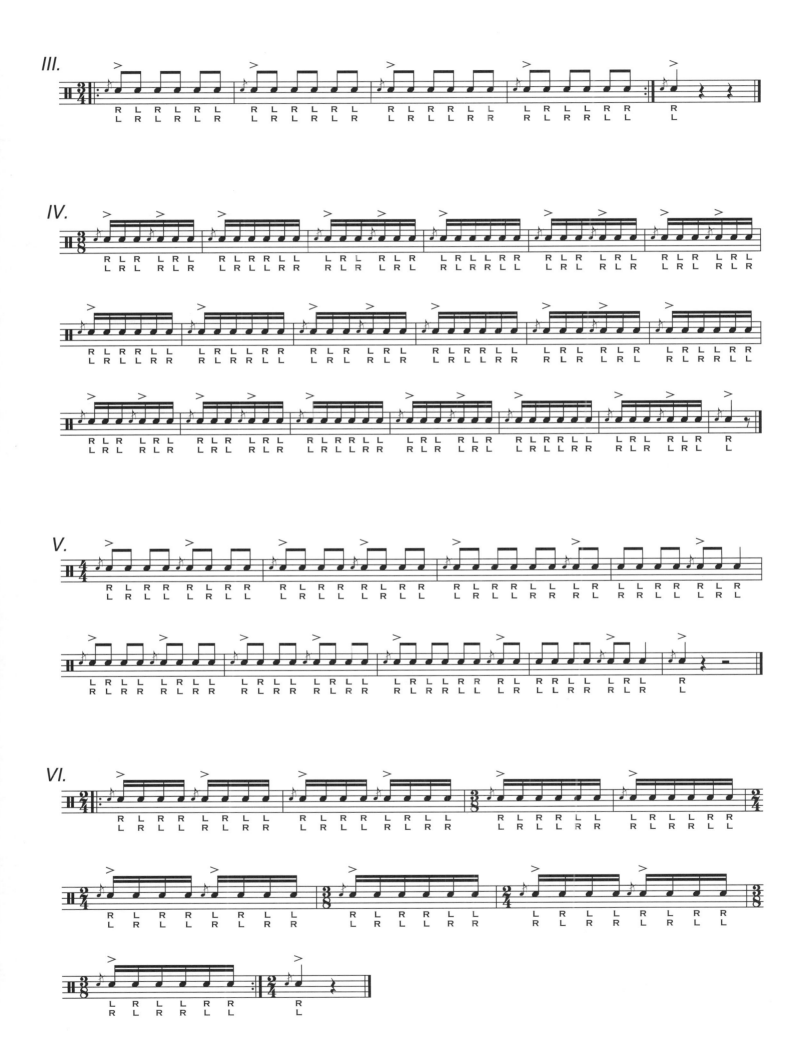

The Flam Paradiddle-Diddle Etude
- perform etude at various tempos and dynamics

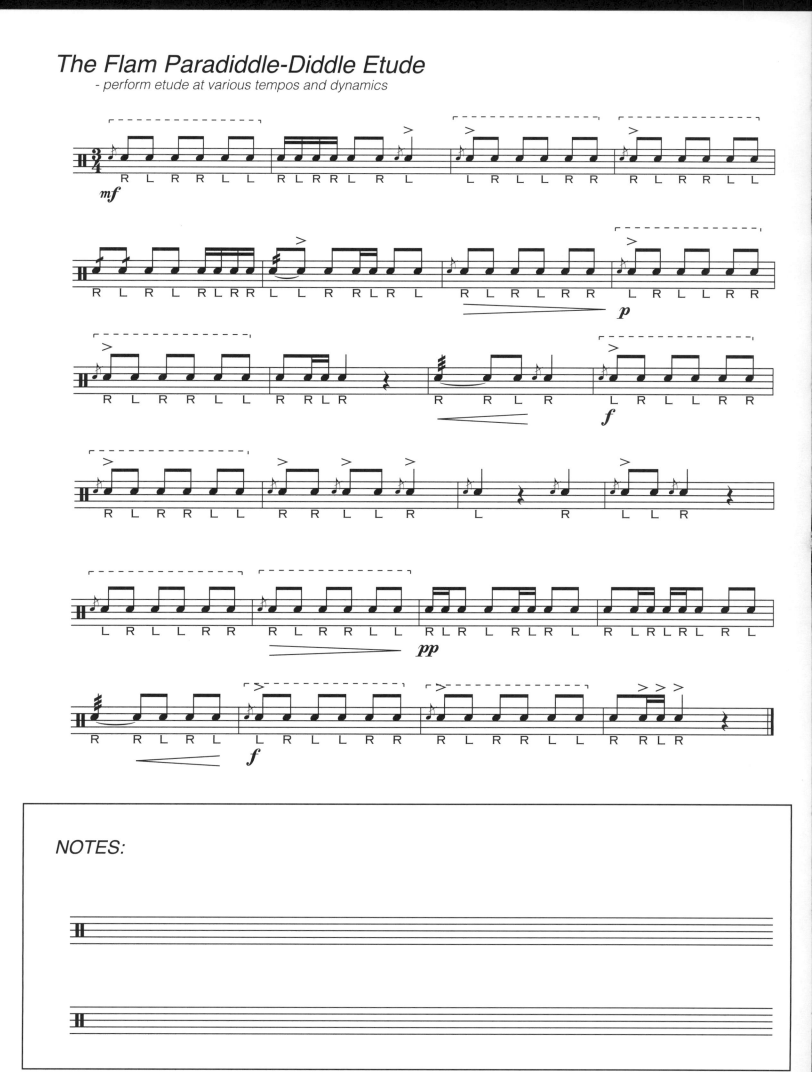

Joe Testa at the helm druring the
SMARTMUSIC Percussion Project recording sessions

The Pataflafla

Also Written As:

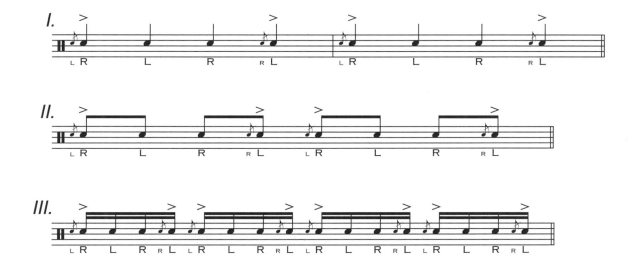

Pataflafla Warm-Ups:

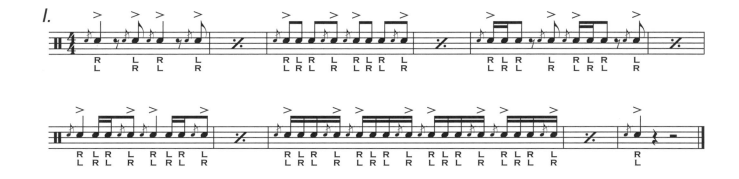

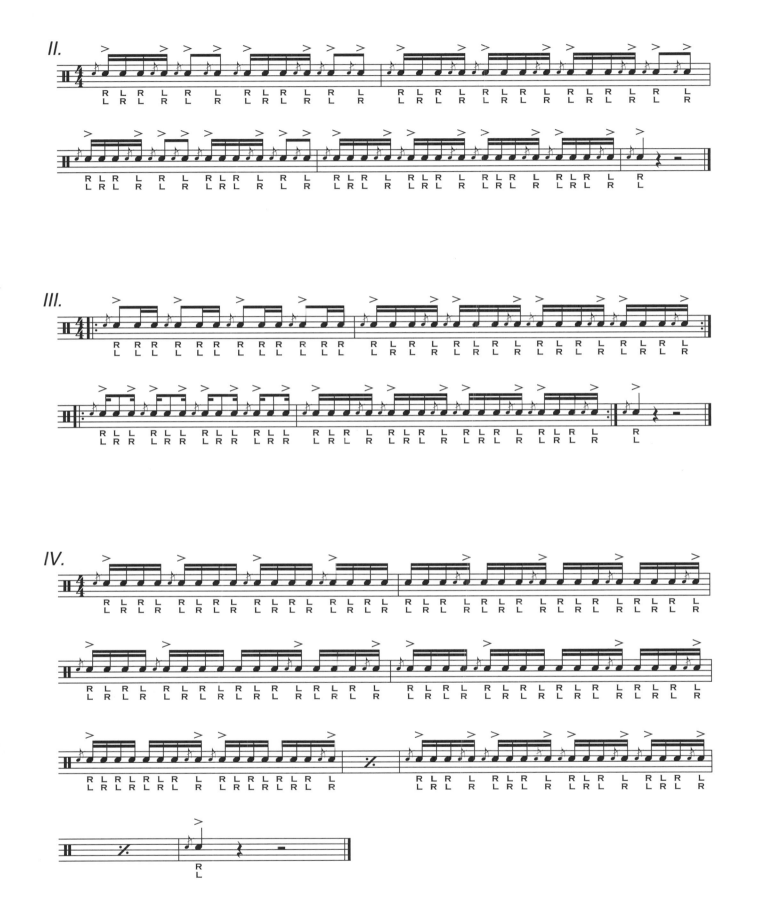

The Pataflafla Etude
- *perform etude at various tempos and dynamics*

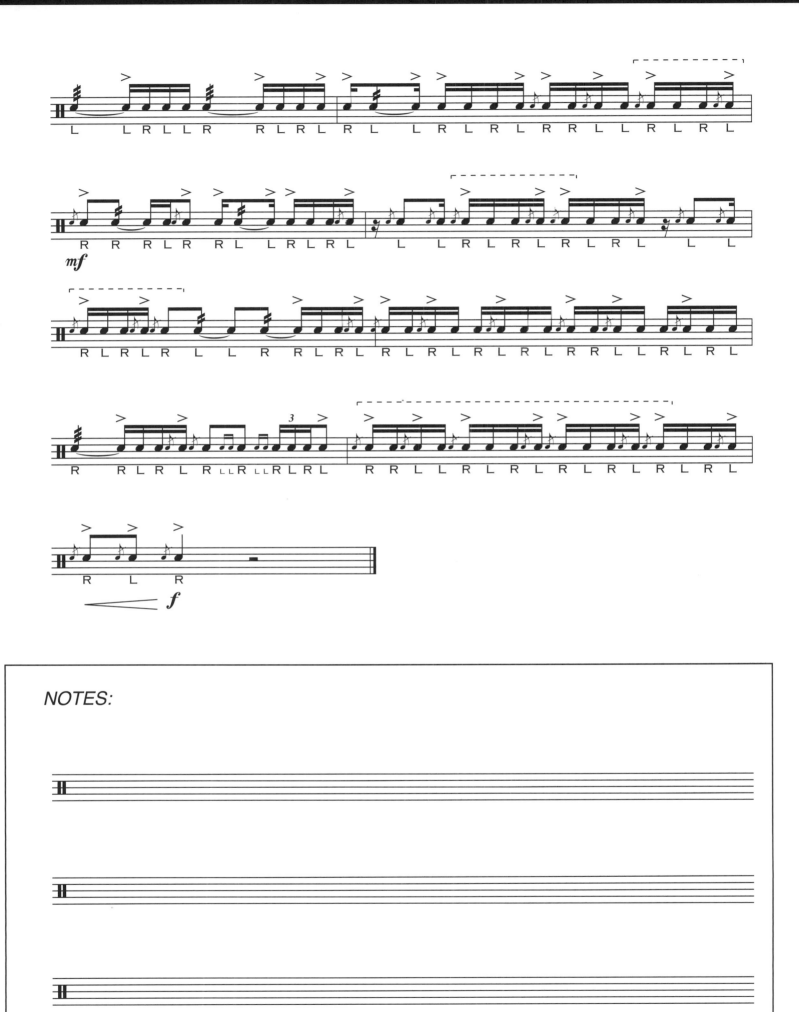

NOTES:

The Swiss Army Triplet

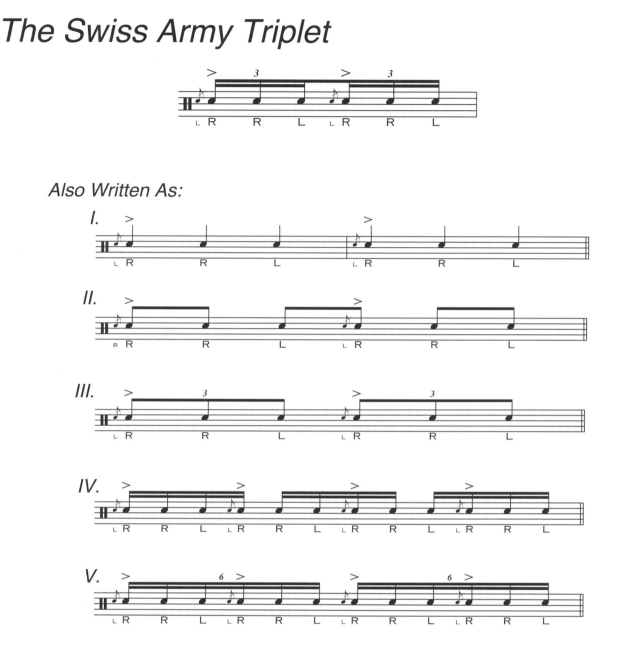

Also Written As:

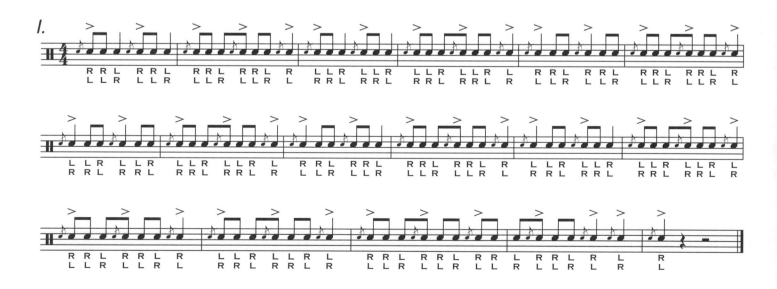

Swiss Army Triplet Warm-Ups:

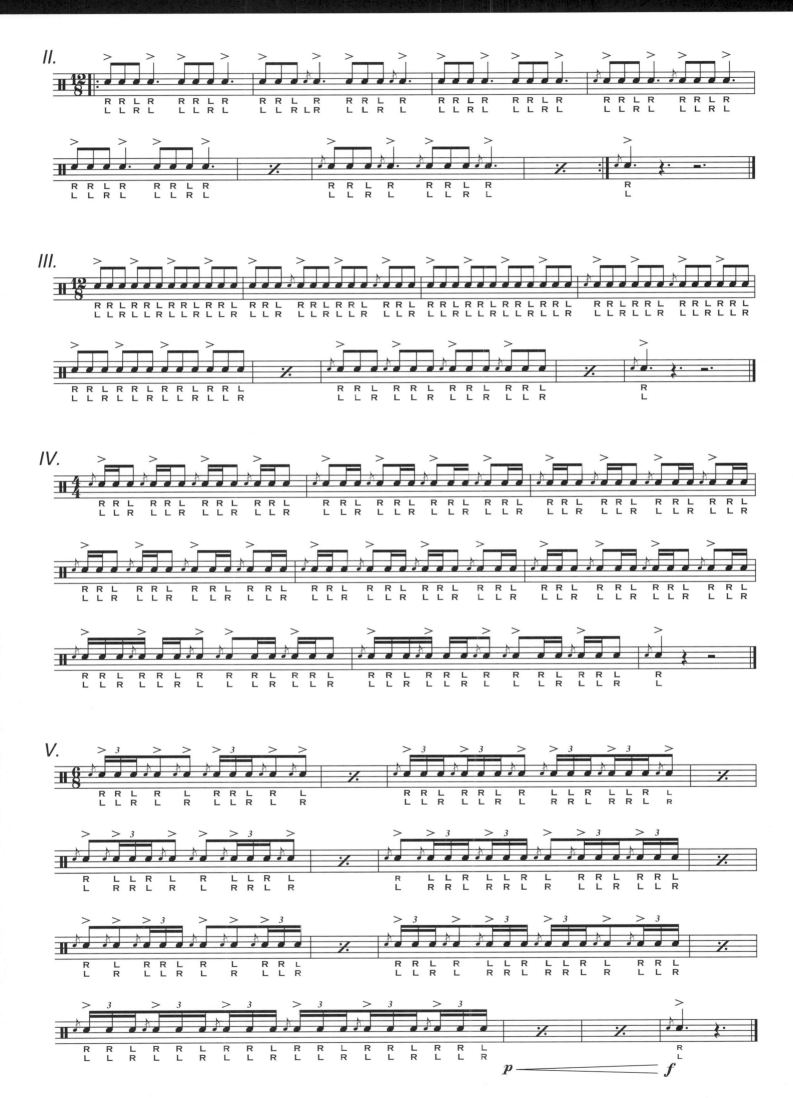

The Swiss Army Triplet Etude

- perform etude at various tempos and dynamics

Steve Murphy editing music for the
SMARTMUSIC Percussion Project

The Inverted Flam Tap

Also Written As:

Inverted Flam Tap Warm-Ups:

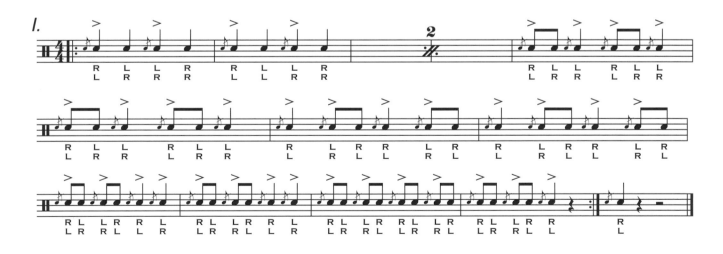

The Inverted Flam Tap Etude
- perform etude at various tempos and dynamics

NOTES:

The Flam Drag

Also Written As:

Flam Drag Warm-Ups:

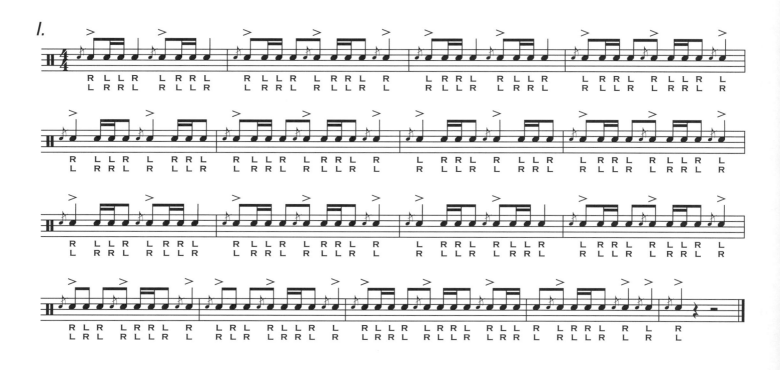

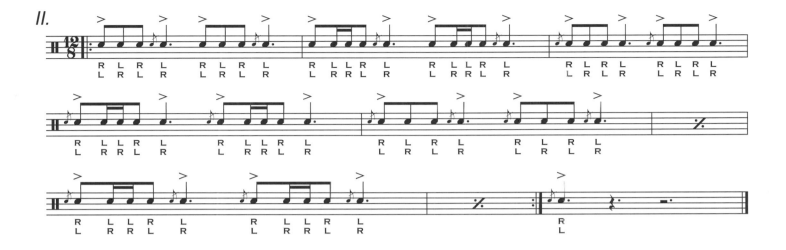

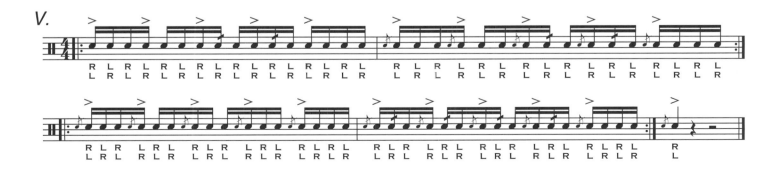

The Flam Drag Etude
- perform etude at various tempos and dynamics

SECTION 4

DRAG *

SINGLE DRAG TAP *

DOUBLE DRAG TAP *

LESSON 25 *

SINGLE DRAGADIDDLE

DRAG PARADIDDLE #1 *

DRAG PARADIDDLE #2 *

SINGLE RATAMACUE *

DOUBLE RATAMACUE *

TRIPLE RATAMACUE *

The Drag *(also known as Half Drag or Ruff)*
Rudiment Included in the Original 26

Also Written As:

Drag Warm-Ups:

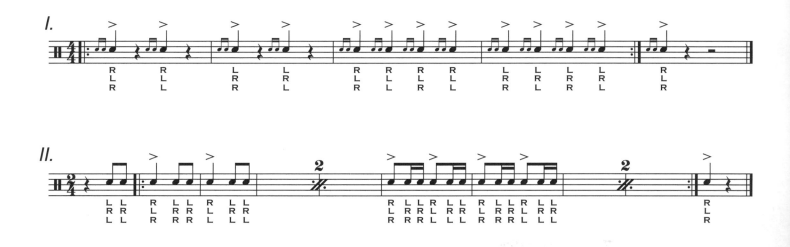

The Drag Etude
- perform etude at various tempos and dynamics

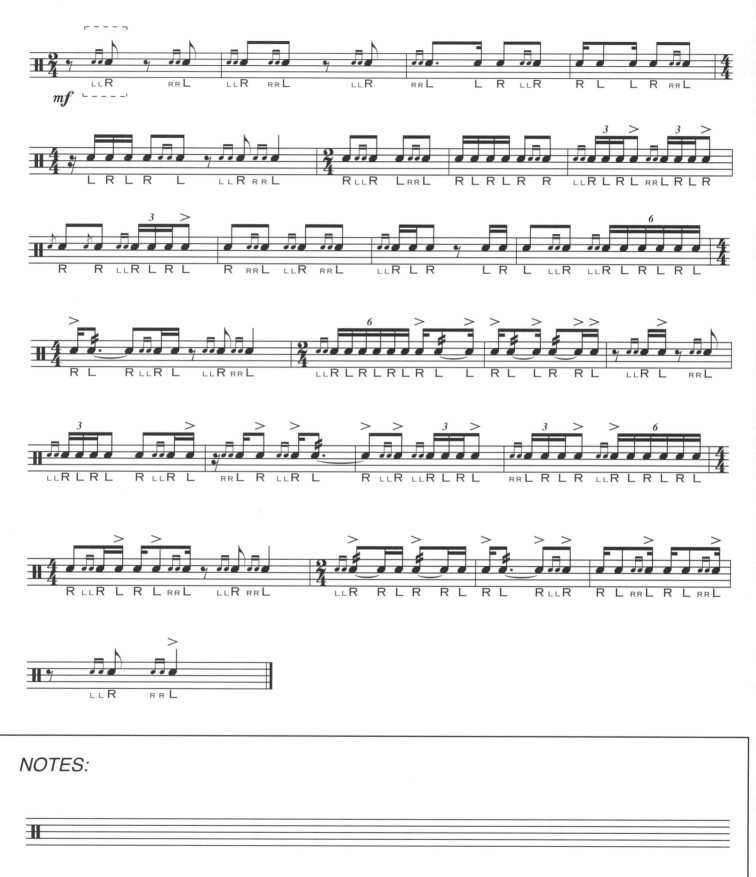

NOTES:

Kit Chatham performing etudes for
the SMARTMUSIC Percussion Project

The Single Drag Tap
*Rudiment Included in the Original 26

Also Written As:

Single Drag Tap Warm-Ups:

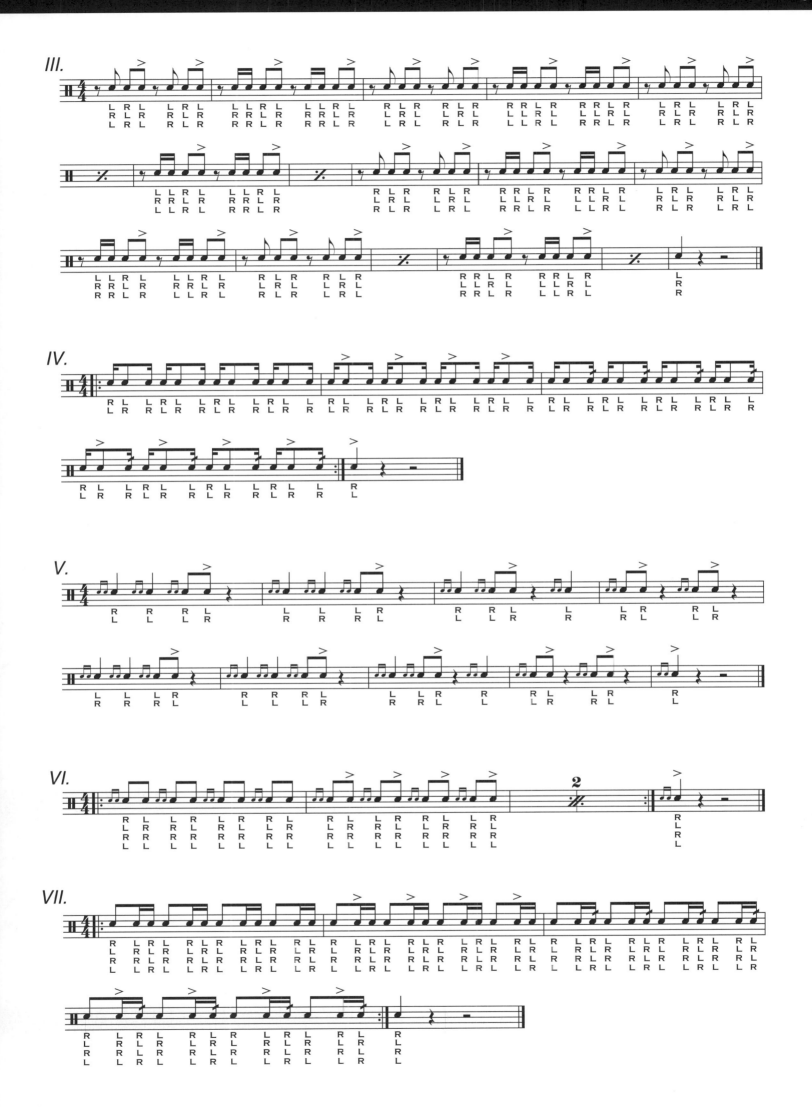

The Single Drag Tap Etude

- perform etude at various tempos and dynamics

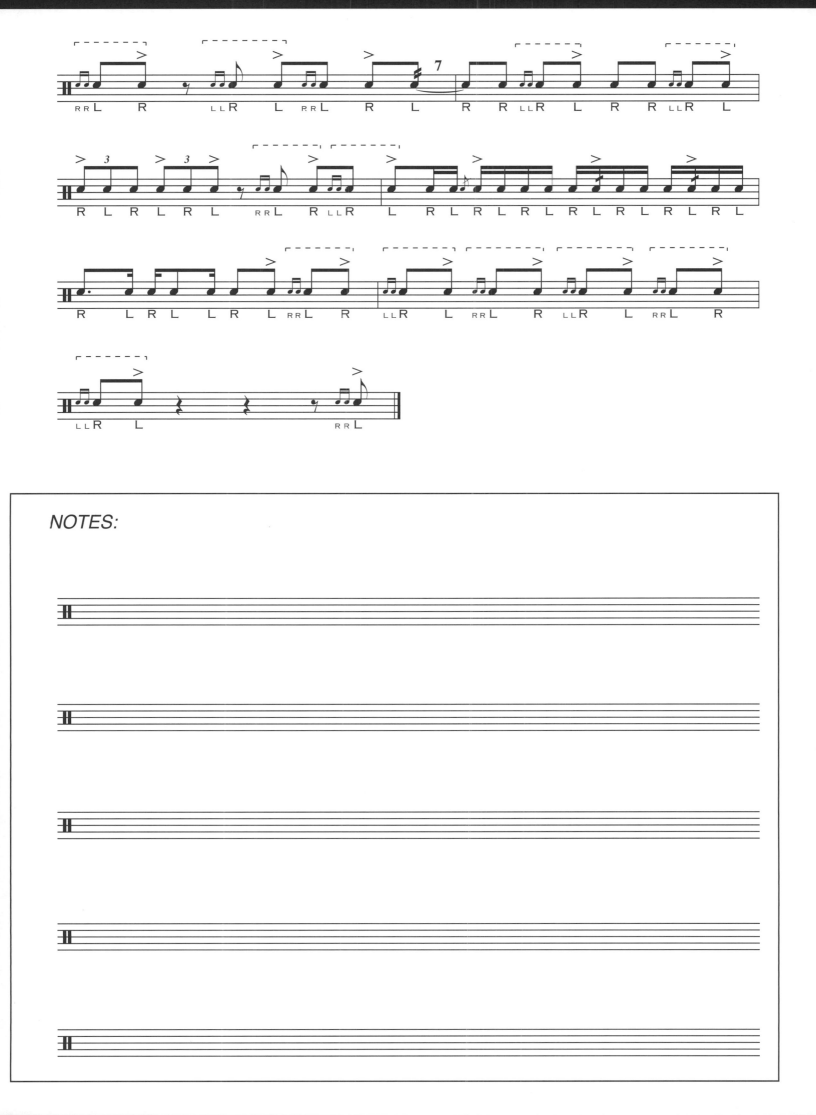

NOTES:

The Double Drag Tap
*Rudiment Included in the Original 26

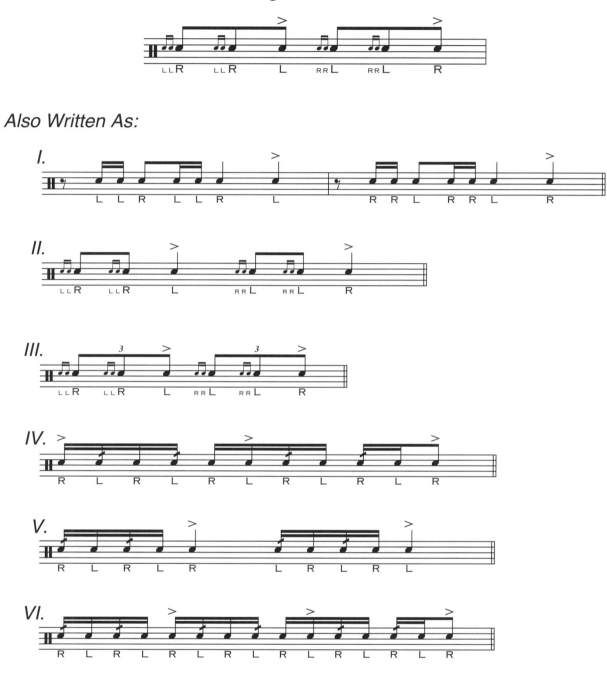

Also Written As:

Double Drag Tap Warm-Ups:

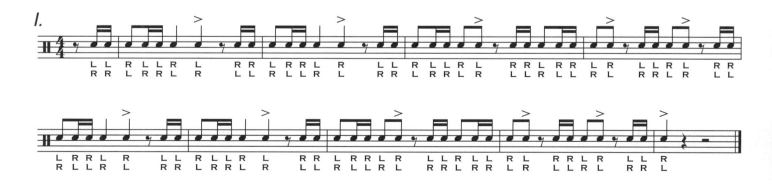

II.

III.

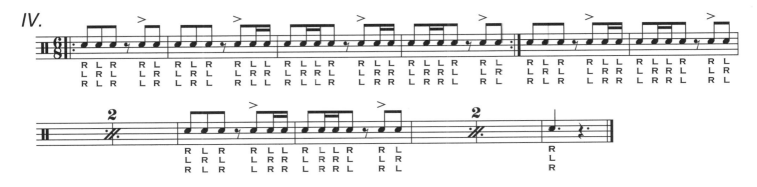

IV.

V.

VI.

VII.

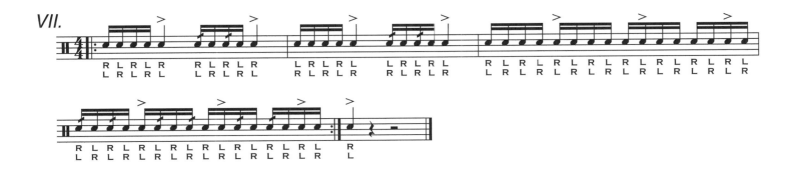

Double Drag Tap Etude
- perform etude at various tempos and dynamics

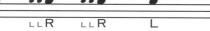

The Lesson 25
Rudiment Included in the Original 26

Also Written As:

Lesson 25 Warm-Ups:

The Lesson 25 Etude
- perform etude at various tempos and dynamics

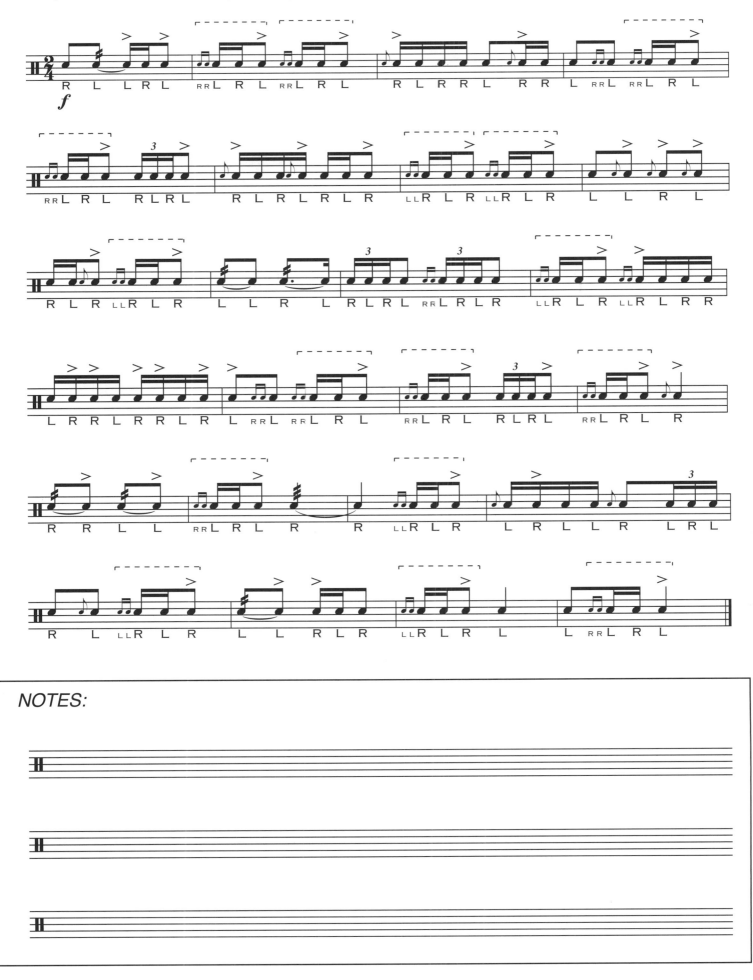

NOTES:

The Single Dragadiddle

Also Written As:

Single Dragadiddle Warm-Ups:

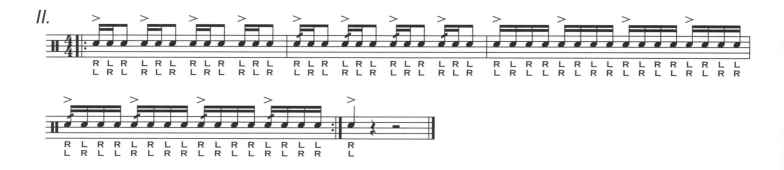

The Single Dragadiddle Etude

- perform etude at various tempos and dynamics

The Drag Paradiddle No. 1
*Rudiment Included in the Original 26

Also Written As:

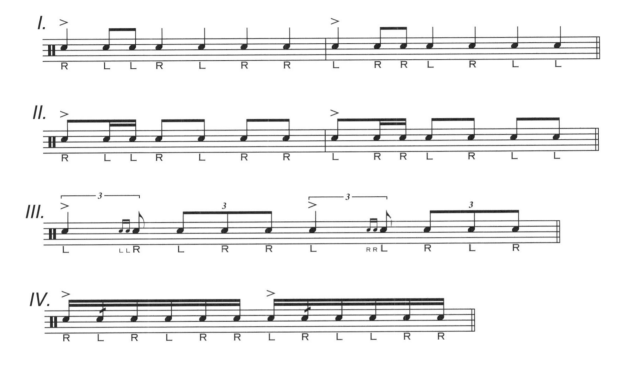

Drag Paradiddle No. 1 Warm-Ups:

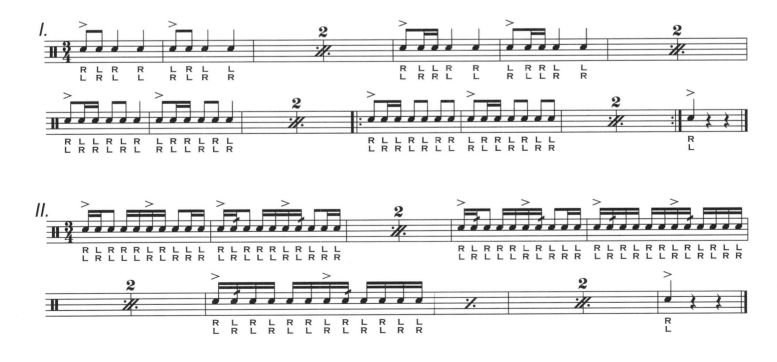

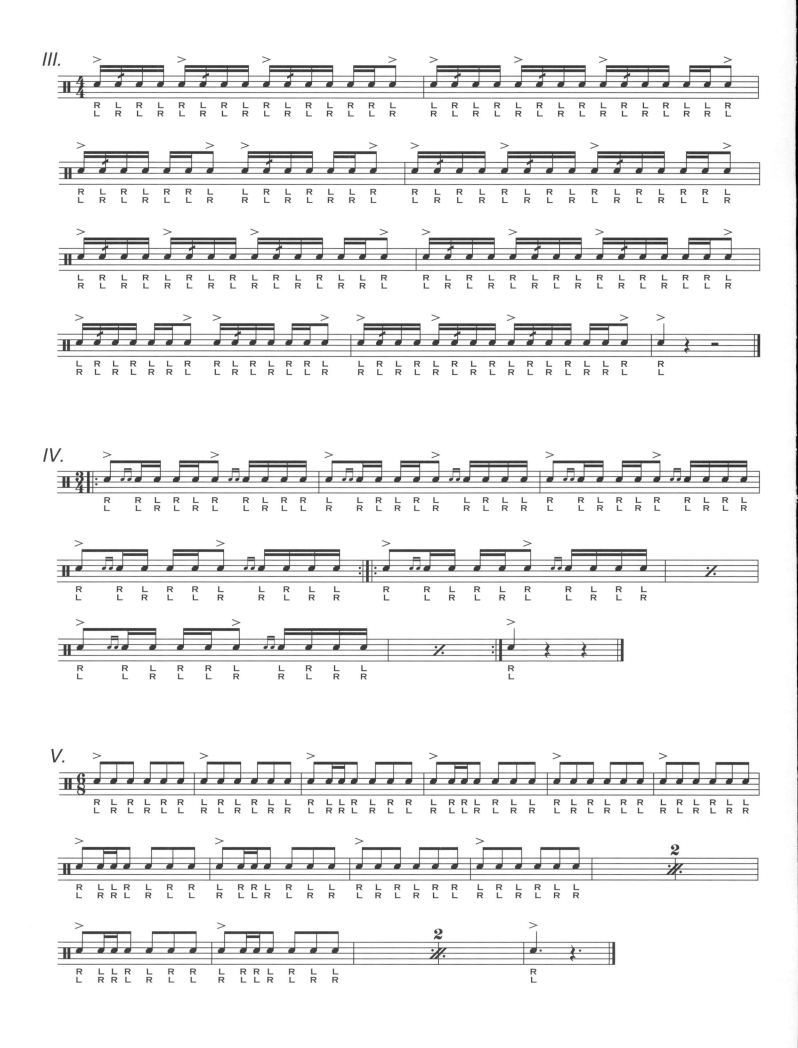

The Drag Paradiddle No. 1 Etude

- perform etude at various tempos and dynamics

The Drag Paradiddle No. 2
Rudiment Included in the Original 26

R LLR LLR L R R L RRL RRL R L L

Also Written As:

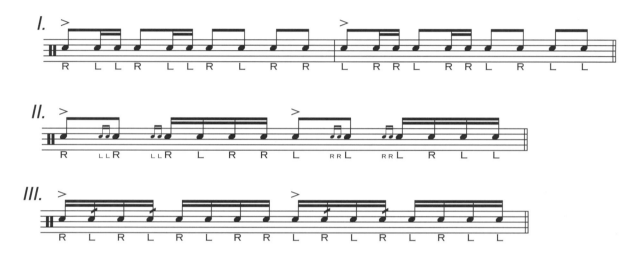

Drag Paradiddle No. 2 Warm-Ups:

The Drag Paradiddle No. 2 Etude

- perform etude at various tempos and dynamics

The Single Ratamacue
*Rudiment Included in the Original 26

Also Written As:

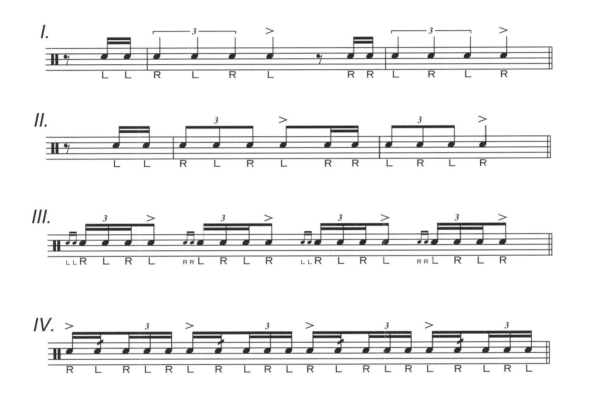

Single Ratamacue Warm-Ups:

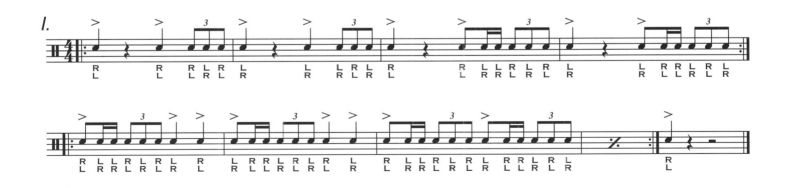

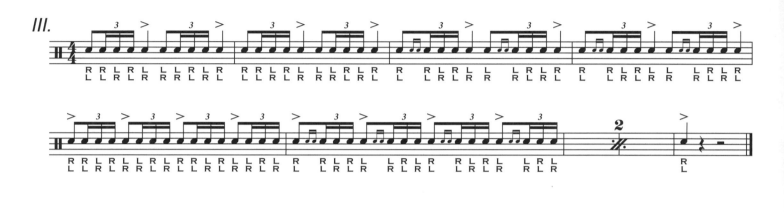

The Single Ratamacue Etude
- perform etude at various tempos and dynamics

The Double Ratamacue
Rudiment Included in the Original 26

Also Written As:

Double Ratamacue Warm-Ups:

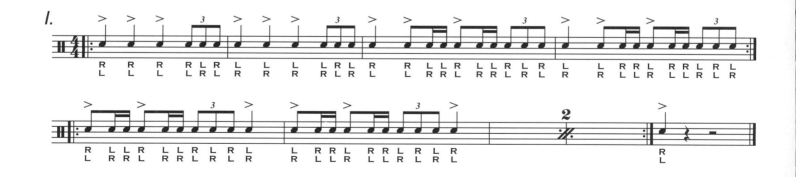

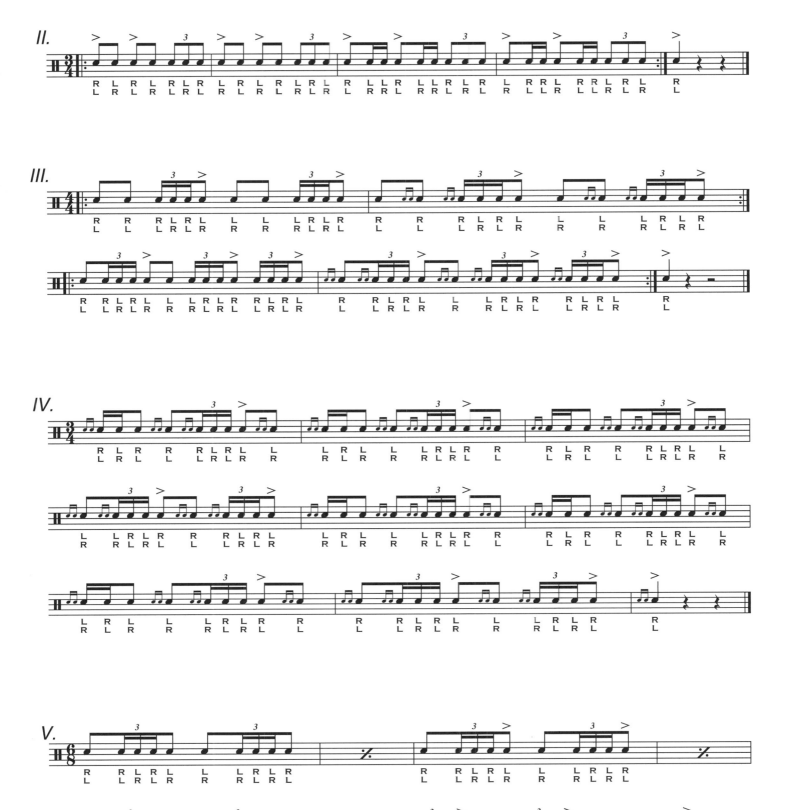

The Double Ratamacue Etude

- perform etude at various tempos and dynamics

The Triple Ratamacue
*Rudiment Included in the Original 26

LLR LLR RLRL RRL RRL LRLR

Also Written As:

I.

II.

III.

Triple Ratamacue Warm-Ups:

I.

The Triple Ratamacue Etude

- perform etude at various tempos and dynamics

NOTES:

Practice all of these
etudes using
SMARTMUSIC and
even listen to them all
being performed by
Kit Chatham

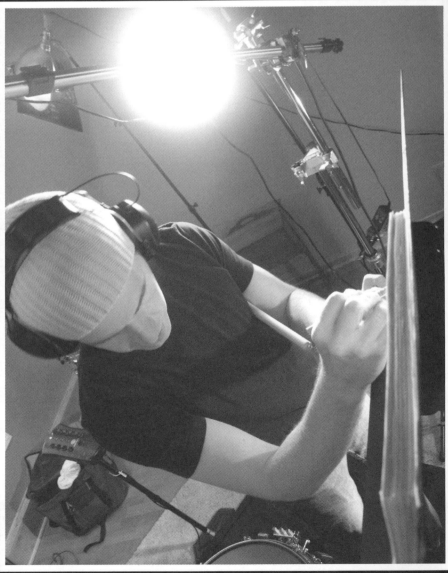

www.PrincipalPercussionSeries.com